Egerton K. Laird

Incidents of Travel in South Africa

Being an Account of a three Month's Tour in the Cape Colony...

Egerton K. Laird

Incidents of Travel in South Africa
Being an Account of a three Month's Tour in the Cape Colony...

ISBN/EAN: 9783744755825

Printed in Europe, USA, Canada, Australia, Japan

Cover: Foto ©Andreas Hilbeck / pixelio.de

More available books at **www.hansebooks.com**

*From Affect [of?] Mother
Elizabeth Land*

INCIDENTS OF TRAVEL

IN

SOUTH AFRICA.

BEING AN ACCOUNT OF A

THREE MONTHS' TOUR IN THE
CAPE COLONY,
ORANGE FREE STATE, NATAL,
AND A RIDE INTO ZULULAND.

BY

EGERTON K. LAIRD.

[*PRINTED FOR PRIVATE CIRCULATION.*]

PREFACE.

My object in having these letters printed for private circulation is, that my mother, up to a few days before her death, shewed such a keen appreciation of them, and of anything connected with my wanderings in the Cape Colony and Natal, that I thought her family and friends might like to have some slight record of the tour.

The pleasure my mother took in hearing descriptions of the various places I visited, arose more from the invariable interest she evinced in anything that concerned her children than for any intrinsic merit in the letters themselves. I need hardly add that they remain practically word for word as written on the spot.

Birkenhead, Christmas, 1881.

CONTENTS.

CHAPTER I.
                                                        PAGE

Castle Hotel, Dartmouth—A Gale—" Citron "—Sister Catherine 1

CHAPTER II.
" Kinfauns Castle," at Sea—In the Tropics—Madeira—Funchal—The Convent—In a Sledge—The Portuguese—The Southern Cross 5

CHAPTER III.
" Kinfauns Castle "—Rolling—Porpoises—St. Helena—Landing under difficulties—Jamestown—Longwood—Napoleon—A Muscular Christian—Jacob's Ladder 12

CHAPTER IV.
Royal Hotel, Cape Town—True Zoedone—" The Only Jones "—Table Bay—The Docks—Sir Bartle Frere 21

CHAPTER V.
Royal Hotel, Cape Town—Rowing—Sea Point—Wynberg—The 99th—Table Mountain—The Table Cloth—A Review—Luggage—House of

Assembly—Everlastings—Constantia—A Sunset—The Malays—Vegetables—The Flats...... 26

CHAPTER VI.

Craven Club, Kimberley—The Veldt—The Karoo—The Climate—The Paarl River—Hext River Pass—Beaufort West—The Coach—Mules—Farm Houses—A Kaffir Location—Richmond—An Irish Renegade—Mud-Larking—A Boer—A Happy Family—Matrimony—A Lively Span—A Sea of Mud—Jagersfontein—The Modder 41

CHAPTER VII.

Craven Club, Kimberley—Kimberley—Bricks—Africanders—Salaries—A Liberal Government—Coursing—A Kimberley Landlady—Kimberley Lodgings—The Mine—A Kimberley Pompeii—The Star Diamond—A Claim—Diamond Washing—Illicit Diamond Selling—A Steam Navvy—A Failure—A Human Hive—A Kaffir Fight—The Basutos—An Amusing Story 61

CHAPTER VIII.

Bloemfontein—A Curious Conveyance—Frost—Bloemfontein—The African Bund—Boers—A South African Oxford—Educational Capabilities—Broken Rest 81

CHAPTER IX.

Ladysmith—St. Andrew's School—Coffee Drinkers—The Orange Free State—Free State Boers—The Kaffirs—The Transvaal—The "Fortnightly Review"—Climax of African Travel—Absalom Van Reenan's Pass—The Rising Sun 89

CHAPTER X.

Ladysmith—A Sanguine Woman—"My Level Best"—Rest Camps—Newcastle—Ingogo—Sir George Colley—Mounted Infantry—A Humiliating Treaty—Lang's Nek—Amajuba—Aylward—Confusion—A Charge of Cold Steel—Short Service—A Guerilla Warfare—Boer Tactics—Lady Florence Dixie—Sir Garnet Wolseley—Sir Hercules Robinson—The 41st 100

CHAPTER XI.

Pietermaritzberg—Magnificent Weather—Transport Waggons—Ladysmith—Wild Firing—A Hard Couch—Off-saddling—A Hairless Animal—Zulu Beer—Zulus—Gay Parasols—Kraals—Helpnakaar—Tinned Meats—A Three-Cornered Tot—Zululand—Rorke's Drift—Isandhlana—Natural Landmarks—The British Lion—A Fog—A Zulu Guide—Fugitives' Drift—V.R.—Zulu Beauties—Umgeni Falls—Maritzberg—Durban—Abraham and Sarah 120

CHAPTER XII.

Natal Club, Durban—A Tempting Offer—An Ant-Heap—The Kaffir Boom—A Sugar Mill—"Kitty"—An Unpleasant Night—Flies—The Botanical Gardens—Swallowing the Leek—Sir Evelyn Wood—Confederation 149

CHAPTER XIII.

Fern Cottage, Port Elizabeth—Blinders—A Passenger Basket—Settled—A Gale—A Narrow Escape—"All's Well that Ends Well"—East London—A Dangerous Game 160

CHAPTER XIV.

Fern Cottage, Port Elizabeth—Algoa Bay—Surf Boats—Bronker's Spruit—The "Vineta"—"H. M. S. Pinafore"—Wool Washing—The Zwartkops—A Large Store—Imports—Commercial Tariffs 168

CHAPTER XV.

Port Elizabeth—Elephants—Grahamstown—An Episcopal Squabble—A Meaningless Act—Sevenoaks—A Fine Panorama—Sabbatarianism—"Snuff and Butters"—Ostriches—A Bogus Company—Ostrich Farming—Vanished Prestige—"The Pretoria"—A Fine Run—Plymouth .. 180

Incidents of Travel in South Africa.

CHAPTER 1.

Castle Hotel, Dartmouth,
April 29*th*, 1881.

Reached here all right, after a tedious journey of eleven hours from Birkenhead; too sunny and glaring for a railway journey, though pleasant enough for a start by sea. The Midland line through Derbyshire is, I think, a snare and a delusion, as the transient glimpses of fine scenery are spoilt by the frequent tunnels, and just as you are enjoying a bit of mountain glen, there comes the scream of a whistle, and a whirl into darkness. Up to Bristol my nephew (who was going to join the "Britannia" at Dartmouth) and myself had a carriage to ourselves, with the exception of a little girl with uncanny wild eyes, who got in at Cheltenham; glad she went so soon. At Bristol a real crush of seven in a smoking carriage, and by the "Zulu," a fast Great Western train to Dartmouth. I find that the ship is crammed; two besides myself in the cabin. Weather like summer, so beautiful and calm.

"Kinfauns Castle,"
At Sea, <i>May</i> 2nd, 1881.

Written at an angle of forty-five degrees or thereabouts.

Had intended writing a detailed account of the voyage so far, but, owing to the weather we have had, I've been hardly able to hold my head up, much less hold my pen, or retain hold of anything that I partook of; so all the beauties of Dartmouth I had thought of dilating on, must be left to imagination. We started with a fair breeze and a calm sea, but, alas! next day a gale sprung up. The storm has raged ever since, though now it is in our favour, and gradually quietening down. Yesterday we had squalls of nearly hurricane force; the ship behaved well under the circumstances, but she is a lively boat and very light, which causes the screw to jump about more than it ought. We are due in Madeira to-morrow, and the letters have to be posted by 8 this evening. We have made a good run—308, 312, and probably to-day 320 miles. They say we are to run to Cape Town in nineteen days. As to the passengers, I have not seen much of them; out of eighty first-class, only about twenty at meals, so I cannot judge much about them Of my two cabin companions, one is a very nice young fellow, and a good sailor; he is going out to the Cape to find something to do; the other is a youth of eighteen or so, a Cockney Jew of the most unstained pedigree, probably going out as a haberdasher's assistant; he subsists on lemons, citrate and biscuits, and I shall name him "Citron," for though his diet is lemons and his face of that hue, yet "Citron" is more euphonious. "Citron" has never been at sea before, and does not like what he has seen of it. We, on principle, both for his own benefit and our own, insist on his getting up on deck, where he remains all day, and lies there huddled up in rugs; he talks not, neither does he eat, and at 8-30 goes to bed and sleeps sound till the morning; so is very inoffensive, yet when he gets well will, I think, be amusing. As to the others, apparitions appear on deck, and as hurriedly go to the side, and "over the garden wall," as they say in the play, hang their heads; there are of course some exceptions—people who smoke and are happy. I hope after Madeira we may have fine weather, and that we may settle down to the ordinary routine of ship life, for if this goes on much longer, we shall be in bad plight. I do not improve as a sailor; in fact, am rather worse, and if it were not that hope springs eternal in the human breast, and visions of calm seas and still atmosphere float before one's eyes, I should turn back at Madeira. There are five young men on board going out to seek their fortunes; four of them have been shockingly ill, and when one was asked if anything could be done for him, he said, "Fetch me a little arsenic." There is a Sister Catherine on board, who, as usual with all these sisters, is in blooming health, and looks physically, and doubtless is also mentally, robust. One thing about the members of sisterhoods is that they appear to enjoy the good things of this life, even if they have some of the crosses.

CHAPTER II.

IN THE TROPICS.

"KINFAUNS CASTLE,"
AT SEA, *May 5th*, 1881.

When I last wrote, before reaching Madeira, I, like most of the passengers, was in the throes of sea-sickness; now we are in the tropics, and the heat makes one very disinclined to write; still it is calm, though broiling between 80° and 90° in the cabin; in the sun do not know what it is. We are just on a line with Cape Verde, and in fact so near that the water is green. We are doing our thirteen knots an hour—320 miles yesterday and 320 to-day. Little or no wind; no steamers sighted; in fact, the voyage is devoid of incidents; there is nothing particular to note; all voyages much the same, and the log I kept in the "Great Britain" is a sample of all, so I will not repeat. There is plenty of musical talent on board, and to-night there is to be an entertainment in the second class, and the first give one on Tuesday. Athletic sports are to take place next week. Cricket and boxing go on daily, as the passengers are all well now, and appetites rising. Citron. now he is well, has been re-christened "Jacob;" he is a most amusing youth; he is going out to Cape Town as a clothier, and is always saying "Well, we *are* a happy family." Like all Jews, he knows the value of money; bought things at Madeira, edible and otherwise, and retailed them at a profit among the second-class passengers. We reached Madeira on the 3rd, having run 1,226 miles in under four days, which, considering the weather, was very good. About two hours before reaching the Island, we passed a group called Desertes, and they certainly appeared to be well named, as they are very barren, and the soil, I hear, is chiefly composed of sand, but the inhabitants grow and export an immense quantity of onions. The first view of Madeira is certainly very fine, and I daresay seemed more so, as after even four days at sea the sight of any land is refreshing. We ran along the coast for some time before reaching Funchal: the hills terraced with vines, which are grown to the height of 2,000 feet, the darker green of the hills higher up, with the small estancias nestling amid clumps of trees, afforded a very pleasing and enchanting view; and at this time everything is looking at its best in its Spring garb. Funchal itself is an open roadstead, and is only a harbour by courtesy. The usual boats came off with the chattering and noisy boatmen, divers who disappeared into the clear water after threepenny bits, and vendors of various goods clamouring out their wares. After the usual inspection by the medical officer, three of us landed, and instantly walked through an avenue of splendid plane trees to a square, where we bargained for three ponies to take us up to the Convent, situated about two miles up the hill at the back of the town, from which a fine view is to be had; the road was next to perpendicular, or more correctly I should say, path, as there was no room for wheeled vehicles, and paved with small sharp flints, worn in some places smooth with the runners of the sledges; how the horses kept their feet I know not. It certainly is as pretty a ride as I have ever been, the whole way bounded by gardens attached to the houses, which are built in terraces; and intermingled with the lovely green of the vines, stretched over trellis-work, were masses of brilliant geraniums, westeria, bourgainvilleas, and numerous creepers and flowers of the most varied colours hanging down the walls in festoons. As we ascended we left bananas and semi-tropical vegetation behind, and came to avenues of oak trees all in full leaf, and as we got further up, to pine woods, the aroma of which was most refreshing after all the horrid smells of the steamer. Amidst these latter woods is situated the Convent, from the terrace of which the view is to be had, and, taking all things into consideration, as fine a one as ever was seen. Below, the Bay, with its sparkling blue waters, the four huge ironclads of the Channel Squadron, the "Minotaur," "Agincourt," "Achilles," and "Northumberland," lying at anchor; then the white and, at this distance, clean-looking town, the houses gradually rising up with their lovely gardens; behind, the mountains dark and frowning, with jagged peaks of every shape; lower down, the vines more beautiful than ever, and fertile valleys between some of the higher mountains. There appear to be no large woods, but numerous clumps of trees, so we certainly had every combination to make the panorama a perfect one. The best of the whole was the coming down; we three got into a sledge on iron runners; two men guided the sledge, and down we flew at the rate of eight or nine miles an hour, and in parts, when the men stood on the framework with one foot and guided it by the ropes attached to the end of the runners in front, we must have gone at the rate of fifteen or twenty miles; at least, we came down in ten minutes, and simply flew; the motion is divine; but if any flints were out of place, or any impediment in the way, you would go such a howler, that I do not think I shall tempt Providence by going again : ladies go up in sledges pulled by bullocks, slow but sure; it is no wonder the flints are smooth and slippery as ice with the large traffic that goes over them. The flowers are wonderful, red geraniums of huge size, lilies, roses, gladioli, and numerous others, of brilliant colours, that I do not know the names of; then as to fruit, oranges, bananas, pines, nuts, strawberries, loquats, a small delicious fruit with a slight acidity of flavour, in fact, every variety, as, owing to the different heights the fruits are grown at, the climate varies. We were the only adventurous three that did the view, the others lounged about the town. It is late in the season, and in the town the sun was very hot. The Portuguese here appear a lithe active race, always squabbling and fighting over the unfortunate passengers. We tasted some Madeira, like dark sherry, without the brandy in it. I hear the vines are doing very well this year, after a long time of suffering from disease. The four ironclads looked splendid, and it was a pretty sight to see the small boats sailing and otherwise dancing over the waves, for a ball was being given on the "Agincourt," and in consequence there was a deal of going to and fro.

We sailed at three, and since leaving have had much better weather. On Wednesday we passed one of the Canary Islands, but did not see Teneriffe. The last time I saw the peak was when we passed it in the "Cordillera," in 1870.

May 10*th.*

Passed the line last night; on the whole have not had it so hot; 90° in the cabin; not seen so many flying fish as usual, or animal life; too soon for albatrosses and Cape pigeons. We are having glorious moonlight nights, and moonlight in the tropics is most enjoyable; almost light enough to read by, yet without the glare and heat of the sun. The Southern Cross is seen in all its beauty, the pointers brilliant as ever.

CHAPTER III.

ROLLING.

"Kinfauns Castle,"
May 15*th*, 1881.

I posted a line at St. Helena; this, if all's well, will be forwarded from Cape Town. I am writing it now, as although we are rolling in a fearful manner, from the heavy south-westerly swell coming from the direction of Cape Horn, yet the surface of the water is smooth; and as the captain generally anticipates head gales from here to the Cape, I had better write while I can. We are out of the tropics to-morrow, and on the whole have had an enjoyable ten days; not too hot; calm as it ever is at sea, and it has been pleasant gliding over the slightly undulating ocean, with just a curve of white foam sent up by the steamer, to show off to perfection the intense blue of the water, and with a glorious summer sky above. At night, owing to the moonlight, it has been particularly agreeable; the air balmy; and there is no doubt a soft—I was going to say velvety—feel about the air in the tropics that one finds nowhere else. The other day, as we were sitting under the awning, we heard a sudden shout, as if something was in sight, and sure enough there was, a little ahead of the steamer, a shoal of porpoises, in crescent shape, quite a mile long, going at a great pace through the water. It made one feel quite envious to see them splashing and jumping about in their mad career in what looked the cool clear ocean; but the one consolation to us poor melting mortals was the thought that, owing to one's experience in the bath in the morning, the temperature of the water is as high as the atmosphere. Before we had reached the crescent, they had all disappeared, or we should have gone right through the middle of them.

CAPE TOWN, *May* 20*th*.

As I anticipated, I was not able to add to this till I was once more on *terrâ firmâ*, as we had shocking weather for the last two days—strong south-east winds and heavy head seas; in our light condition, even with 450 tons of water-ballast, we pitched and rolled in a frightful manner—worse than in the Bay of Biscay. We made, on the whole, a capital run, as we arrived in Table Bay last night at 6, or in round numbers—excluding eight hours and ten minutes at Madeira and St. Helena—in nineteen days and twenty-two hours. As St. Helena is nearly twelve hours out of the direct road, it was first-rate going, the distance being 5,984 knots, which is, roughly speaking, 300 miles a day. But I must hark back, as I have said nothing about St. Helena. We reached there last Friday. It certainly, from the sea, has a most rugged and barren exterior, but if you look inwards up the rifts or ravines, you catch glimpses of verdure-clad mountains and wooded slopes; in fact, the sterile outer ranges might be supposed to shelter the inner ones from wintry blasts, if one did not know that the climate is mild and equable. St. Helena is certainly of volcanic origin, and, like all such islands, if there were only water, would be capable of producing anything; and this island has always been celebrated for vegetables, fruit, and live stock generally, and formerly was a great place of call for steamers and ships, and also whalers of the Antarctic region to replenish with provisions, and restore life into scurvy-stricken crews; but owing to the Suez Canal, the number of vessels has so materially diminished, that thousands of the inhabitants have emigrated to the Cape Colony and Natal. There is no harbour, and in bad weather the landing at Jamestown, the capital, is a matter of great difficulty; in fact, the day we landed, though it was calm—always of course allowing for the Atlantic swell—we had a rather dangerous landing, as there is no pier of any kind, nor are you, as at Madeira, shot on to the shore on the crest of a wave, and pulled up before the next one rolls in; but you have to make a jump out of the boat at a slippery step, which if you miss, there is no hope for you, as by that time the boat has gone down several feet lower, with the peculiar up-and-down motion that comes from the treacherous ocean; and if it were not for the friendly hands of a native, stuck out to assist passengers in distress, you would indeed fare badly.

Eight of us went ashore together, the only party that intended to do *the* sight, the only or rather the chief one that makes and will make St. Helena for ever celebrated—Longwood—the place where Napoleon was for five or six years imprisoned by the English Government.

We had three ladies in our party; four of us had intended going, but at the last minute a gentleman asked us to take his wife and two ladies, he being a great invalid, so we asked another of the male sex, and we went ashore and secured two carriages, the only two on the island for hire. Longwood is nearly five and a half miles off, and mostly up hill; so, as we had no time to lose, we started at once, and rattled through the streets of the capital, which is built in a ravine, and if they had very heavy rain, I do not know how the town could be saved from being washed out to sea, as it consists of houses, with a church here and there, dotted along a huge culvert; there are a few more pretentious residences, with gardens attached, as if to show there is some green thing on the island, for the sides of the hills that surround Jamestown are apparently composed of cinders, but if you look up the valley at the end, you see the well-cultivated hills.

The whole population of the island is about 6,000, of every variety of colour and nationality; and its area is 47 square miles.

After leaving the city, we slowly ascended in terraces to the height of about 2,600 feet. We had some exquisite views, and as we neared Longwood, we had a magnificent sunset, and almost before the last rosy tints had died away from the topmost peak, we decended the other side, to see the full moon sending its silvery light through the dark pines that surround the last home of the Great Napoleon. Never have I seen such moonlight, and it certainly seemed a pity to go into the house, and to be shown by the light of a candle the rooms in which the great commander lived and died. All the furniture and everything of interest is in Paris, and there are nothing but the bare empty rooms to see; they are kept in good order, and, though small, look comfortable.

One cannot, of course, realise what must have been the feelings of such a man, exiled to such a lonely isle, and to such a lonely ridge on that island; but one can hardly help feeling sorry for the man, and doubly so, if, as they say, the Governor treated him rudely, and he suffered from cancer; in fact, that is what some reports say he died from. How he must have fretted his soul away! I have read, as if nature could not allow such a man to die without a convulsion of some sort, that on the 4th of May, 1821, the island was swept by a most tremendous storm, which tore up all trees by the roots, and about six in the evening, Napoleon, having pronounced " tête d'armée," passed for ever from the dreams of battle.

Yet, after the feeling for the man is laid aside, what a relief to Europe that he was fairly placed out of the way of endangering the peace again; for had he only been interned in some fortress on the Continent, the various nations could never have felt secure.

I am glad we saw Longwood by moonlight, and so bright that we could easily have seen to read. The original tomb is in a little ravine, a plain white slab surrounded by cypress trees, and near to a crystal spring. As all the world knows, his real tomb is in Les Invalides, in Paris.

The cacti tribe of plants seem to flourish on the hill side, and there were some wonderful flowers. Geraniums grow wild, but the vegetation was, I thought, poor.

We nearly missed the steamer, as we had taken over the three hours to do the journey, but the captain gave us a little law; if not, we should have had to wait for a month—pleasant prospect without clothes or money. The wretched boatmen stopped a short distance from the "Kinfauns Castle," and refused to row unless we paid more money than we had agreed upon; but, fortunately, there was a muscular Christian amongst the passengers, who said he would knock the boatmen into the sea if they did not row on at once, and as he looked capable of doing what he threatened, we were propelled alongside the ship.

I was congratulated when I found out that Jacob had not raffled my clothes and belongings, as that was the prevailing idea of my fellow-passengers, who thought that he could not have resisted the temptation of making something out of our prolonged absence.

A former steamer of this line left two passengers at St. Helena, they not turning up at the time fixed for starting. The captain, when he reached Cape Town, finding a steamer going there at once, sent all their goods and chattels back to St. Helena; as chance would have it, the "Orontes" troopship came in a day after they had been left behind, and took the two passengers to Cape Town, so they passed their goods *en route* to the island. Fancy their disgust on arrival at Table Bay.

The barracks are on the top of a hill, and one way of getting up to them is by Jacob's ladder—699 steps. St. Helena is, in fact, a series of hills, with no large plains or even considerable valleys; a jumble of peaks shot up from the sea at some time or other. This is a poor account, but it is nearly a week since I was there, and all my ideas and recollections have been rolled out by the "Kinfauns."

CHAPTER IV.

TRUE ZOEDONE.

Royal Hotel, Cape Town,
May 23rd, 1881.

I am penning this at the City Club, with my back to a hot fire, with blue flames suggestive of frost in England; here, I imagine, of a north-west wind. It is difficult writing at the Club, owing to the incessant conversation going on amongst Colonials, every word of which I should like to hear, because it is about the country of which I come to learn as much as I can. Toasting your toes at the fire, and seeing a gentleman holding his face to it, as he is suffering from neuralgia, sounds funny in Africa, where one's ideas of the climate formed at home are burning sands and brazen skies. The three first days here were truly delicious. A bright sun, not too hot, air more exhilarating than zoedone, more like that of Egypt in winter, yet without the glare, as the prevailing soil here is a dark red, a lovely blue sky, and such surroundings! However, of these more anon. The reason for a fire, and I may say this letter, is a north-west wind and rain that we have had all day, rain such as you only get in the tropics or in Africa. But now a lovely starlight night, and the mountain looming in the distance; let us hope it will be fine to-morrow for the 24th, as it may be the last time this date will be of any importance, if Mr. Gladstone carries out his policy in these parts.

I have said enough about the voyage; half the passengers were Jews, and out here nearly every other person you meet appears to be of that nationality; Solomons and Cohens equal Browns and Smiths at home. At St. Helena, the chief firm—in fact, "the only Jones," as they say—is Solomon, Moss & Gideon.

There is no doubt the first view of Table Bay is a fine one. We arrived about five o'clock, so everything was heightened by the rays of the setting sun; but at any time the semicircle of the Bay, with its blue waters terminating in white surf, the glistening white beach, the ranges of the Blueberg, and, further on, the still higher peaks of the Drakenberg, must always be a fine panorama, let alone the celebrated Table Mountain, that rises like a wall, with its grand upright cliffs, behind Cape Town, to the height of 3,800 feet, the Devil's Peak, and the Lion Mountain, which Trollope thinks resembles one of Landseer's lions. To me, the absence of vegetation is a fault, yet at the end of the driest summer known for years, excuses can be made if any are wanted; yet, after all the harbours I have seen, I doubt whether any town has such a grand background. Fusiyama, as seen from Yokohama, is more sublime; but then, you may say, that that sentinels a country, because it rises in the centre of the largest isle of the empire of Japan, while Table Mountain does duty to a small straggling town of 30,000; at the same time, it is one of the causes of the smallness of the population of the capital, as, owing to its close proximity, land is so scarce that rents are abnormally high. What strikes me as usual on landing at an English colony as compared to those of other nations, is the enterprise shown by the inhabitants — at Madeira for instance, with great natural facilities — nothing done for the accommodation of shipping. Here a dock that will take in thirty or forty ships, and sixteen acres in extent, and more in course of construction. Owing to slight rise and fall (only five feet), no need for dock-gates; but the "Kinfauns," of 375 feet, steamed in and berthed alongside a wharf with ease. Table Bay, Simon's Bay, and Delagoa Bay, however, are the only harbours on this coast, and one may almost say—with the exception of those on the north coast—in Africa. Algoa Bay, Mossel Bay, East London, and Port Natal, are only harbours in name. The real outlet for Natal, the Transvaal, &c., is a bay near Delagoa, about which Mr. Gladstone and the Portuguese had a dispute as to whom it belonged; it was put to arbitration, and, as usual, given against us. Why we did not buy it I know not, because the Portuguese will not—perhaps cannot—do anything in the way of improving it, and Delagoa Bay is a sink of iniquity morally, and commercially a failure, and is to the Cape Colony what Malaga is to England. The more one sees of the world, I am convinced it is a mistake for second or third-rate powers to hold colonies, as nothing is done for the general good. If they could be taken legitimately and with the consent of the people, let France have Tunis and England Egypt, because I believe that what has been done may be done, and there is no reason why, under powerful and enlightened governments, North Africa might not become what it was when Rome was at its zenith—the granary for half of Europe; and with England dominant in the south, where would the great Sahara be? But I am getting on one of the burning questions of the hour, so must stop.

I have been staying with one of the members for Cape Town, who, I think, is rather against confederation, but he quite appreciates Sir Bartle Frere as a master-mind, and different to the general run of Governors, who are, and perhaps rightly, at the beck and call of the Home Government. If Sir Bartle had been allowed his own way, I thoroughly believe he would have founded a South Africa worthy of the name; but the Sprigg Ministry is out, and a nondescript one in, and Sir Hercules Robinson a moderate safe no-opinion-of-his-own man; in fact, a model Governor rules the roast. What these changes will end in doing for the Cape, time alone will show.

CHAPTER V.

ROWING.

Royal Hotel, Cape Town,
May 26*th*, 1881.

As you will have heard in my last letter, I reached here on a Thursday. On the Friday, while at lunch, young B— turned up, and was naturally glad to see anybody from England; and while walking down one of the streets, I met H—, late of the "Defence," who looked none the worse for his march to Mount Prospect, though he came too late for the fighting. I went down to the boat-houses to see B— cox'ing a six-oared boat for the Regatta to be held on the 24th—fine strong athletic-looking fellows.

Saturday was another lovely day, bright sun, yet a delicious atmosphere, cool and bracing, thermometer about 55° in the morning, and 60° or 70° in the day. I gave up one or two letters of introduction, and in the afternoon went again to the boat-houses, and saw five or six crews start—not that I took much interest, but we had a splendid view of the Bay from the pier, and it certainly improves on acquaintance. Whichever way you turn, you have mountains. I dined with the B— brothers in the evening; they live in a nice small house, one and a half miles out, near Sea Point, a capital situation, and the tramway runs past the door. We had a walk before dinner, over a common very like Hoylake; there is also a racecourse and stand, a lighthouse, and low bungalow kind of houses.

On Sunday, at 8-30, I went by train to Wynberg, to spend the day with Mr. F—; it is only a short distance. When the train reached its destination, it was raining and blowing furiously; a pony carriage met me at the station. The coachmen here are generally Malays, who are always great at boating, fishing, and horses. Maynard Lodge is a fine place, with magnificent trees—such oaks—and they, with willows, firs, and Australian gums, appear the principal trees. There is a charming house, furnished with every luxury. After breakfast church was mooted, but there were blinding showers and a gale of wind; in fact, at times the gusts were so heavy that Mr. F— thought his trees would be blown down, and we stayed at home, talked, and had a fire lit; all rooms furnished in the latest style—dados, oak chimney-pieces, with niches for china, &c.; there is also a billiard-room, and a large one, with polished floor, always ready for dancing.

The gardens consist of several acres, but the lawns are not looking at their best, as, owing to the dry summer, everything has been burnt up, but grass and vegetables begin to grow in the late autumn, and though the trees have lost their leaves, they will soon bud again. Wynberg is a lovely place—miles of pine woods, with splendid views of fine undulating country; then what are termed the Flats—a broad expanse of level land between Table Bay and Simon's Bay. Doubtless at one time the sea covered them—in fact, a rise of a few feet would do so now—and beyond, a fine range of mountains. View very extensive, and, owing to the clear atmosphere, things appear much nearer than they are. We examined all the various pets; plenty of fowls of all sorts, horses, and English cattle. After lunch, it cleared up, and Mr. F—

and I took a stroll through the woods, and meeting the Colonel of the 99th, now under canvas, we went into the mess-tent, and had a long talk. In the evening the governess and I went to church, in spite of the wind and rain. Mr. F— is a member of Parliament, so I had interesting talks with him, but will not trouble you with all the various matters we discussed. All are agreed that even if peace with the Boers is patched up, it cannot be permanent; but here you hear far less about the affair than in England; no "specials" to spread false news for the pleasure of contradicting it in the next issue. Nobody thinks there will be the slightest difficulty in travelling, and people are daily arriving from all parts; in fact, we are a long way from the seat of war, and little or no interest appears to be taken in it.

Diamonds and feathers are real subjects of interest. There is such a mania for keeping ostriches, that many who have a little plot of ground, instead of growing vegetables, keeping cows, and a few sheep, go in for birds, and the consequence is that things are nearly at famine prices. Mutton, which used to be 2d. and 3d. a pound, is 9d. to 11d.; a cauliflower 2s; and fresh butter 4s. a pound—in fact, hardly to be got—and other articles of food as dear.

Monday set in a regular soaker, most unfortunately, as I had intended to drive to Simon's Bay, and lunch on the "Boadicea," but it was out of the question; and as there appeared no chance of its clearing up, I came into town. It turned out fine in the afternoon. A friend and myself took a walk to the Saddle that connects Table Mountain with the Devil's Peak, and had a splendid view of Cape Town on one side and Camp's Bay on the other. The rain has already made a great change in the colour of the hill sides, and they are fast assuming a green appearance. Soon after leaving the town, when you get, say, 1,000 feet up, you go through extensive pine forests. We went up the Devil's Peak, but not quite to the summit, as we missed the side where you can clamber up by the help of a chain.

The great thing is, of course, to do Table Mountain, but I doubt whether I shall accomplish it, as the weather is so unfavourable. One thing, I have seen it covered with the table cloth. The summit is perfectly flat, and a white cloud has been resting on it more or less all day, the curious thing being that above, the sky is clear of clouds, and, as I have read, the white cap is smoothed off like a well-dressed peruke. The summer is the usual time to see this wonderful phenomenon, as then the southerly winds prevail, but owing to the unsettled weather of late, the wind has been in all quarters.

From the sea, when the table cloth is on, the mountain must look most curious. On land, it so directly overshadows one, that you cannot see it to perfection. Fancy the surprise of the early navigators seeing from afar the huge solitary rock with its white cap rising apparently straight out of the ocean; for long before you reach Table Bay, you see the mountain.

The town itself is an unsatisfactory one; the streets are wide, but in a shocking state of repair, and though there are some fine buildings—notably the station and some of the large mercantile houses—still the whole has a poor look—not the enterprise of Melbourne, though it is a fairly active town.

Tuesday was, luckily, fine, and I was awakened early by the bugles, drums, and bagpipes of the various troops. At 12 there was a grand review on the parade-ground, a very brilliant sight, heightened as the whole was by the brightness of an African sun. The place itself is most advantageous; at one side one had glimpses of the Bay; on the north the Fort, with its ramparts all covered with green turf; and on another, under the shade of avenues of pine trees, were massed the spectators, lighted up by the gorgeous colours of the Malays, who go in for the most startling colours, red, yellow, and green; then the natural surroundings which I have described before, make Cape Town parade-ground on a gala day a particularly fine spectacle. The troops marched and countermarched, and saluted the Queen with three *feux de joie* and three cheers, and then marched past. Sir H. Robinson was away, but Lady R— was there—a woman of enormous dimensions— a veritable Hercules.

In the afternoon the regatta was held, and went off well; the Bay alive with white sails flitting here and there; the piers crowded with the usual gay native throng, all chattering and laughing. Two bands—those of the 91st and 99th—discoursed sweet music, so there was every combination to make the regatta a success; and it was, monetarily and otherwise. On Wednesday I tried to compress luggage for eight weeks into thirty pounds—not much—but that is all one is allowed up country, except you pay 1s. or 1s. 6d. a pound extra; and in post carts they will not take more, pay what you will. I have bought a carpet-bag, as they are said to stand wear and tear better than anything else. You are allowed to take coats or rugs, in fact, anything you can carry loose, free, and I hear it is very cold up country. In the afternoon I went to spend the evening with a gentleman who lives two miles out—a large house facing the Bay, and a fine avenue of oaks leading up to the Table Mountain range. We had a stroll of an hour or so, and then came in to tea.

Thursday was, unfortunately, a wet day. I had intended going—as it was a holiday, for they keep Ascension Day here as one—with B—, a ride across the Flats to Wynberg, to have lunched with the F—'s, then to Constantia to see the vineyards, but it was not fit. I never knew such rain—all our expeditions put a stop to. The "Orontes" arrived with troops from the Mauritius, but only stayed a few hours, so I had no time to go off and see the captain.

On Friday it did not actually rain, but that was all that could be said about it; the streets are in an awful mess, about a foot deep in liquid red mud, and no attempt to clean them; pavements of the most primitive kind; and in the summer the dust must be something quite "too-too." I wore my Lewis's warranted waterproof boots that I bought before I left England. Their double were in the window, with fountains playing around, and goldfish swimming among them; as I think they are really waterproof, I intend to take them up country.

In the afternoon I went to the House of Assembly, as the Speaker, who I was introduced to at the Club, told me it would be worth my while going; it is a long room, with a reporters' gallery at one end; the Speaker's chair, mace, &c., as in the House of Commons, and facing the Speaker's chair is the Speaker's gallery, and place for the public. I saw no ladies or ladies' gallery. There was a very interesting debate about the Basuto War, and I heard the Premier, Mr. Scanlan, make a statement; he is also Attorney-General, and being only a lawyer, he has disgusted the barristers. But a Premier out here can select what office he likes. He spoke fluently, and to the point. I was quite struck by the way in which all the members spoke with such apparent ease—no hesitation. After staying an hour, and seeing a friend I knew, we went a walk up the hill at the back, inspected the new reservoir, and wandered among the woods. You cannot go wrong, and if one was only a good walker, you could easily spend a week or ten days here. Flowers in thousands springing up after the rain; masses of a small pink one particularly noticeable; many of them are everlastings—Cape Town and neighbourhood being celebrated for the latter. At 5-30 we went again to the House for an hour, and heard a member called to order by the Speaker, though decidedly more orderly than the majority of the Home Rulers. After dinner I went to the Club, and then to the House; they were in committee of supply, but a gentleman advised me to go late, as some honourable members usually wax warm, and there are two Irish members who are particularly rowdy; they have billiard-tables and a bar in connection with the House.

On Saturday B— and I went by an early train to Wynberg, hired a trap and drove to the Constantia vineyard, three miles off. We went at a great pace through avenues of oaks and firs; on one side were the Flats, then the white beach and the boundless ocean, and on the inner side huge forests trending away till lost in blue haze, and towering above all, the rugged sides and peaks of the Table Mountain range. Constantia is in a valley, but the vineyards extend some way up the sides of the mountains. They are sixty acres in extent. They are not now looking to advantage, as the vines have just been pruned, but the surroundings are beautiful, and the houses and buildings neat and clean. We tasted some of the wine—too sweet, like all colonial wines, for my fancy. We examined the arrangements for making the wine, bottling, &c.; and we drove back and went over the camp of the 99th. This unfortunate regiment was sent for at a moment's notice during the Zulu War, from Halifax, where it was then stationed; they arrived too late to be of any use; the head quarters were then removed to Bermuda, and after the affair at Amajuba, they were sent for, and are now camped out at Wynberg, having for the second time arrived at the Cape when all further need of them was over; however, I suppose this is one of the glorious uncertainties of war. We then walked slowly through the endless avenues to the house where B—'s father lived for some years. The young man pottered about the old familiar spot, showed me the pond in which he used to swim boats, the shop were he purchased lollipops, the house where the gardener lived — a man who was bold enough to marry a black woman—and how the first infant was white and the second black, and other interesting details. We then returned by train, and had a most lovely sunset, the colouring simply gorgeous—one of those wonderful ones where objects miles off stand out clear and defined in the golden light, which, on changing to red, caused the numerous ships lying in Table Bay to appear as if they were floating on a crimson sea. The effect on the mountains I did not notice, as all my attention was directed seawards. "Too brilliant to last," said I, and sure enough soon after rain came down in torrents, and it is dull and heavy to-day.

Just returned from the Cathedral service, which was nicely done, the anthem, "Lift up your heads, oh, ye gates," being finely rendered; a large congregation; not a handsome building—like a barn.

On the whole, considering the wretched weather,

I have had a good time; undoubtedly the scenery grand, and Wynberg a most entrancing spot. The sylvan glades would have gladdened the heart of the late Lord Beaconsfield, who said that though mountain and lake scenery might pall on one, trees never could. Then the study of the various natives is most amusing, the dress, &c., and never shall I forget, on the Queen's birthday, the gorgeous attire of the Malays and other sightseers not of European extraction, and of the dark crowd that lined the parade-ground, picked out, as I read yesterday in the paper, with spots of scarlet, yellow, and blue, like an English cornfield. The simile may not be a good one, but the poppy and the golden grain are as lovely a contrast as there is in nature. Then again, the market is a picturesque sight, owing to the varied hues of the vendors— black and brown faces, and the Malays with their whitey-brown complexion, dark eyes, and magnificent teeth. Then the motley buyers; fancy our old cook, Mrs. T—, now a greengrocer, arrayed in a green dress, starched till it looks as if the wearer had a steel crinoline underneath, and in shape resembling a Popoff ironclad, a red shawl around her shoulders, and a brilliant handkerchief over her head and ears. Like the Japanese, the Malays' taste in dress is so perfect, that colours, to our idea however trying, harmonize in some wonderful way.

As to the fruits, oranges, loquats, apples, pears and lots of others of which I know not the name; cauliflowers three feet in diameter, and such cabbages! The Malays of native races are the best off here—originally imported as slaves by the Dutch, from Java—now, thanks to English rule, free to do as they like, and even to do the British, for they are arrant thieves, but never rob each other; resembling the light-fingered gentlemen at home in this respect. They talk now of having Dutch spoken in the Legislature. Oh, ye gods! and in an English colony this is *since*, as a member told me to-day, the Transvaal business. The Dutch, I believe, in the farming class, outnumber the English, but the coloured natives generally vote for the English, as they hate the former. Even in Java, as I wrote at the time I was there, a species of slavery exists now, and you may imagine what the Boers do; however, the deed is done. Yesterday was a grand market day, and to see the spans of oxen, sixteen in number, and mules, six in number, was novel; in fact, I know not a town where there is more of interest turning up every minute.

When we were on the edge of the Flats, yesterday, watching a farmer with a cart and six ragged horses, leaving the main track and trêking across the apparently endless wild, though in reality making for Somerset West, a place lying under a blue promontory that stood out in bold outline against the dim horizon, one felt that one had seen a life-like representation of what one has often read of—of some settler starting off into an unknown country—for anything more devoid of cultivation or signs of life than the Flats, I know not.

We have very heavy rain to-day, and quite a rough sea. I went to the Cathedral again; a crowded congregation; singing somewhat harsh, and I think the half-caste voices are not as full as the genuine article. Heard a striking sermon on the manifestation of the Spirit.

CHAPTER VI.

THE VELDT.

CRAVEN CLUB, KIMBERLEY,

June 13*th*, 1881.

I wrote a hasty line *en route* to this place, which we have reached in due course, but five days late, so I have missed another English mail; luckily, taking all things into consideration, we have reached here at all. On the whole I have enjoyed it, but it has not been the picnic I anticipated; still the surroundings have been so novel, that it has been interesting. The great lack in the scenery is the want of trees, and the great charm is the clearness of the atmosphere, which makes the horizon appear boundless, except where the Karoo and Veldt have their somewhat monotonous flat broken by a mountain range. Verdure is nearly absent now, but it is the middle of winter, and the dried-up looking grass is in its proper season a mass of green. This is the Veldt which we passed through for the greater part of our time, though in the Free State we had a taste of the Karoo, which is an arid waste, and is a name given to the barren portion of this part of Africa, while the Veldt is a general term for the fertile division; and it is wonderful now to see the thousands of goats and sheep, not to mention the cattle, that appear to extract some nourishment from the dried-up herbage. Horses that are doing regular work, though they are turned out at night into the Veldt, are fed on bundles of oat-straw, which costs 2s. a small bundle, and mealies £5 for 200 lbs.; in fact, horses' keep here is most expensive—40s. a-week under the most favourable circumstances.

After leaving the railway at Beaufort West, the three-hundred and fifty miles to Kimberley lie on a vast plateau 3,000 to 5,000 feet above the sea, broken, as I have mentioned above, by ranges of hills and solitary peaks. The most curious part of the latter is, that they are nearly all, in shape, a repetition of Table Mountain and the Lion's Head and Rump, and Nature does not seem to have been prodigal in giving variety in contour to single peaks, though the ranges are fantastic and diversified enough. The sunsets have been glorious, and we have had moonlight nights the whole way. As I read the other day, there is little of the tender beauty of the pastoral scenery of England, but one is impressed rather by the vastness of the country —12,000 acres a common size for a Boer's farm— and by the grand extensive views whichever way one turns. The air is bright and exhilarating, the nights intensely cold, always hard frost, and ice on the ponds; but then comes the difference to our winter, the sun rises at seven, and the minute he is above the horizon he appears to have great heat, so the ice soon melts, and as the sun rises into the cloudless blue, it becomes hot enough in his rays, though out of them there is always a delicious cool breeze. There is no dampness in the atmosphere, so it really does not feel too cold, though winter clothes are quite necessary. This climate is highly recommended for consumptive people, and doubtless its dryness has to do with it. Though we had no exciting incidents by the way, I will write an account of our eleven days' trip from Cape Town. I did not keep any diary, and Silver's Guides, unless one has come out here as a botanist, astronomer, or settler, are really useless; after all, personal knowledge is the best.

June 1*st*, 1881.

Left Cape Town at eight, by train to Beaufort West, narrow gauge, filthy carriages, only averaged ten miles an hour; they are Government railways, so there is no redress, and charges are exorbitant. We had no rain, though, after the wet we have had, there was no dust. I came by the eight o'clock train that I might see the scenery by daylight, but there was nothing special until we came to the Paarl River. The town of that name is beautifully situated in a valley, lofty ranges of hills on either side, and the river in the centre; it extends for six miles, and appears to consist of one street; it is celebrated for its vineyards and for its magnificent avenues of oaks and firs; it was founded in 1650, therefore is one of the oldest towns in the colony. We passed large ostrich farms, but I must give an account of one later on, so will now merely say that ostriches are ungainly birds to look at.

June corresponds to our December, yet out here it appears to be the month in which young lambs do play; but everything here upsets all one's calculations as to the fitness of things.

We ascended till four o'clock, when we entered

a gorge, with lofty rugged mountains on either side, and a torrent foaming down below. We wound round the gorge like a serpent, till we emerged into the valley of Ceres. The name suggests fertility, but winter is not the time to judge, as the vines are cut down and have only a few yellow leaves on them, and the crops are not seen, though wheat is springing up after the rain. The mountain ranges now became higher, and some were covered with snow. Who would have dreamt of seeing snow-clad mountains, of no great height—say 7,000 or 8,000 feet—in Africa.

We then began to ascend the celebrated Hext River Pass; had three engines, one, curiously enough, in the centre. The curves are very short, and, judging by the steam and noise the engines made, must be, and are, very steep—a wonderful piece of engineering. If you looked out of the window, the first engine appeared as if it were going to run into you. The new moon now appeared; it certainly was a weird, if grand, sight. We stopped at Montague Road, say 3,000 feet up, and had a few hours' rest; had to get into the train at 2.45 a.m.; great difficulty in finding room. There was a coupé, with apparently only one lady in, so into this the guard said I was to get, much as I object on principle to travel with a lone female. As the lady moved, a cry was heard. "An infant!" I exclaimed. "Not if I know it," said I; so I had to cram into another carriage. The night was intensely cold, but the day as hot as ever; the country very barren and desolate, and for the most part only a station-house and a drinking saloon at intervals; the towns, as a rule, fifty miles away from the line.

We reached Beaufort West at 4 p.m.; it is the terminus—339 miles in about thirty hours. We dined here.

Beaufort West is a rising place, as it is from here most of the bullock trains, &c., start to Kimberley, or perhaps the greater number come from Port Elizabeth direction. The streets are wide, planted with trees, water running at the side; the houses are square, and, as a rule, one storey. At 6 p.m. we left in the coach with fourteen passengers, there being really only room for twelve. The coach consists of a vehicle on four wheels, built more for strength than comfort; it has a light wooden roof, and canvas blinds at the sides and ends that you can let down or up. There are four seats, holding three each, three facing the driver and one at the back. There are cushions, and the thing is fairly comfortable, though draughty. The driver gets £15 a-month, and is as independent as all colonials are; the fact is, you do everything for yourself. As to them touching your baggage, it is an absurdity for you to think of their doing so; mine, weighing thirty pounds, I can carry easily enough. It was shoved on the top, without any tarpaulin or covering of any kind, and though it came on to rain, it was too much trouble to cover it up; though £14 for a trip of 350 miles is rather heavy. They do not charge high at the hotels, but the feeding is not *recherché*; however, there is plenty of it, and in this rarified air, one's appetite is good.

There are no roads in Africa; there are tracks, varying from a quarter of a mile to a mile in width, about as even as a Cheshire lane. Space is of no object out here. There is only one bridge— that over the Orange River—the whole way to Kimberley, so none of the gullies, torrents, or rivers are bridged, or rocks or stones removed. Over these latter obstacles you go, generally at a gallop; the effect may be imagined; you bound and rebound like an india-rubber ball, at an angle of 45°. Coaches do upset, but fortunately we did not. We had ten mules, two abreast, to start with. Talk of a whip in London! the drivers here are marvellous; catch the fifth pair of mules on the shoulder or flip a fly out of the first one's ear. A boy runs along with a whip made of hide, for mules take a deal of driving; but they seem to improve as they go on, and are never done up, or give up struggling on, and in my opinion are, on South African roads, decidedly preferable to ponies, more sure-footed, and though they are not so willing and do not trot so fast, yet when a pony is tired he chucks it up, and no beating will get him on. Now, a mule appears too obstinate to succumb altogether, and let him have a roll and a little water for his breakfast, and two hours to browse on the prickly mimosa, and he is ready for another stage, while the horses require a regular feed and rest. We stopped at 10, had a cup of coffee, and on till 3 a.m., when we turned in till 6, and had breakfast. Hard frost, and glad of two coats, rugs, and a muffler; in fact, driving through the keen air at night you want all the wraps you can get. We bumped over the bed of the Buffalo River, at certain seasons half a mile across, had dinner of sardines, &c., at one, to let the mules get their roll and food. The scenery I gave a general description of above, so need not repeat. We drove over one vast plateau diversified by peaks. The farm-houses have always trees about them, three or four acres under tillage, and fruit gardens, for few places are more blessed with fruit at the proper season— grapes, oranges, peaches, apples, &c., in abundance. The farm is generally near a river or well, and the homestead is a one-storied building of sunburnt bricks. The vast plains are the feeding-grounds of the flocks and herds; they are driven at night into the kraals, and let out to roam in the morning. Ducks, geese, and fowls abound, but this is not the time for getting eggs; it is too cold I fancy. Reached Murrayberg, a town of about 2,000 inhabitants, at 10 p.m. on the 3rd, and had a comfortable sleep on good beds till 6 next morning. Left Murrayberg on the 4th, after a cup of coffee at 7. Had a team of ten horses. The mules will now have a rest of two or three days, which they need. On leaving the town all the trees were covered with rime, and looked beautiful in the bright beams of the sun. A small stream we crossed outside the town was covered with ice, and though we had a good team, we had to go most carefully. This will give you some idea of the nightly frost. Breakfasted at 10 at a Boer's farm. Had milk, eggs (for a wonder), bread, and mutton-hash, all for 2s. 6d. These Boers were pleasant enough; they have a large ostrich farm and a great many horses—altogether a prosperous-looking homestead, with the usual garden and enclosure. Further on we passed a Boer's house; no love of the English; all doors closed and window-blinds down, like a deserted village; nobody about; would sooner shoot you than give you a meal. This feeling has increased very much since the fatal peace—fatal at any rate as far as the unfortunate people who have any dealings with them in business are concerned. Of course you always pay for your meals at these farm-houses. Passed a Kaffir location; their huts resemble a low haystack, with a hole in it by which they crawl into the interior; the natives are dirty-looking objects, with filthy blankets.

Arrived at Richmond at 7; a nice clean-looking town; slept the night there. We ought to have met the coach going to Beaufort West, but it did not turn up, and as we had to exchange teams, we had to wait till nearly 1 o'clock, so took a walk about. A very pretty town, with river and plenty of trees, and in Spring the gardens must look beautiful with their blossoms. The jail is the largest building. Two young men here condemned to be hung for murdering an old man they were travelling with—a very brutal case. There is a large export of wool from here. I went to service in the morning. This town is 3,500 feet above the sea, and is surrounded by barren ranges of hills; all the roofs are made of corrugated iron. It was hardly possible to realize that we had gone through the winter scene of yesterday, and now wandering in the brilliant sunshine.

Left at 1 o'clock on the 5th for Hanover. When half-way, and when going, at full tilt as usual, across a deep ravine, the pole broke; fortunately we were only two miles from the town, and the night was moonlight, so we walked in, and the coach followed by slow degrees. I had to sleep on the sofa, and had to wait till 1 p.m. on the 6th to have the pole repaired, when we continued our journey. Hanover is a sleepy kind of town. Wool, as usual, is the chief export. Stopped, at 7 p.m., at a farm-house belonging to an old Scotchman; had a cup of coffee. They actually had paper on the walls, and wooden floors. Drove on right through the night to Colesberg, which we reached at 5 a.m. on the 7th; with great difficulty managed to get something to eat, having had nothing but coffee for sixteen hours. On in an hour to Phillippolis, where we dined at 1 p.m.

A pretty town, with lemon trees and splendid willows, the last we see for some time, as the Orange Free State is very barren and wretched. Met here Aylward on his way home; he is the Irish renegade who helped the Boers all through the war; he ought to be shot. He says that the Boers are not afraid of infantry, but are afraid of cavalry, and are particularly frightened at shells. General Wood, he says, is determined to have the murderers of Malcolm and Barber given up. I hope he will stick to it; if not, a Transvaal fugitive I saw says all will be up and murders will be common. This man said that loyal Boers and Englishmen are regularly boycotted and turned out of their farms, numbers having gone to England to get compensation; but what good, if Mr. Gladstone sticks to the letter he has written on the subject; it certainly is most unjust to these unfortunates.

Had tea at a Boer's house, after having stuck in a road which resembled a ploughed field. Hired a team of passing oxen; with their aid and by dint of digging and pushing the wheels, got the waggon out. It was now dark, the sky clouded, and moon obscured, but some tried to find their way to a farm-house. The driver returned with a span of mules: more digging and pushing, and raining all the time; at last reached the farm. At 11 o'clock started off again, and all went well till 3 a.m. on the 8th, when we stuck fast again, two miles from a farm-house. It was now a perfect deluge, and pitch dark; nevertheless, we had to turn out and push the waggon, being nearly up to our knees in slush. When just as we thought we had reached our destination, the driver found out that he had missed the road. Small blame to him, as when it rains, the Karoo becomes very similar to the track; so for half-an-hour we had to stand in a deluge. At last a cock was heard to crow, and at 6 a.m. on the 9th we reached a farm-house. The Boer would not let us in at first, and when he did we had no change; but he lit a fire, and at last warmed up, and his wife said she would make coffee for us. You have to be most particular with a disagreeable Boer; their impudence is unbearable, considering that this place is where the horses are regularly changed; and they charge a shilling for a wretched cup of coffee, and everything in proportion. At 8 o'clock the old lady thawed sufficiently to say she would give us some breakfast, but this concession was chiefly owing to a gentleman who spoke Dutch, and who smoothed the old lady down. The husband was a very pleasant man, and talkative; he spoke English; the wife owned the poultry, &c., and all we paid for the food, she pocketed; the husband had no say in the matter; he looks after the farm, and the wife the household. The farmer himself was a typical Boer, six feet three at least, with a fair beard, and a good, though wholly expressionless, face; in fact, stolid and stupid, a pipe never out of his mouth. This man has a farm of 12,000 acres, lots of sheep, cattle and horses, yet their house, which was a good type of a Boer's farm, was a comfortless one-storied building. You first enter a room which is always kept as the best, with generally a piano or harmonium in it, but mud floor, and no paper on the walls, the whole place filthy; off this room, at each end, a bedroom; then you enter the living room, and at one end of this is the kitchen, at the other a kind of store-room, and that is all.

The Boers are all musical and devoted to dancing; the best trait in their character is their fondness for children. This man had five of all ages; he played with them and tossed them about; the eldest played the concertina, and the little infant of two years old or so was made to dance; they appeared a happy, though dirty, family; the fact is, they seldom wash, and don't change their clothes for weeks. This man must be well off; all he makes goes to buy more land, worth here from 10s. to £1 an acre. No idea of what we call comforts; hates telegraphs; hates any drains; loves smells, and seemingly thrives on them. This man showed us his rifle; last week he shot four springboks, a small kind of deer, two at eight hundred yards; it was an English rifle, latest stamp; they are educated to be good shots and riders. When a child is born, so many sheep and cattle are put aside for him; at seven he rides a pony, and at eight a rifle is put into his hand. The girls marry at sixteen, sometimes at fourteen, and boys at sixteen to eighteen, and they seem to be suited by the arrangement, judging by the size of the men, and though they have not rosy complexions, they appear healthy enough.

To show how the Dutch hate innovation, one of the Dutch members at Cape Town, the other day, got up to propose that gas should be done away with in the streets; it was no use to them, as they never went out at night except it was moonlight. I mentioned about the drains, in fact they hate change of any kind, but are good parents, and devoted to their old relations; they marry in and in, and this accounts to a certain extent for their want of intelligence.

Some one asked this farmer why he did not cultivate more ground where there was water. "Oh," he said, "no good; I only want to grow enough oats to feed the animals and to cultivate a fruit garden;" in fact, to our ideas they lack energy, but they seem to be perfectly happy, and, like the Chinese, all that they want is to be let alone.

It still rained heavily, so at 1 o'clock, as horses would have been useless, we hired a span of sixteen oxen to take us to Fauresmith, twelve miles off; the driver galloped off to the town and left us to our fate. We had only gone two miles when we stuck in a rut, and all the efforts of the oxen to pull us out were useless. They were a young team, and skipped about like lambs instead of behaving in the usual way of the stolid ox. The chain broke, so some of us walked on in the rain to a farm-house, to try and procure a new one. The Boer was sulky, and would hardly speak, much less lend us anything. Luckily there was a canteen near kept by an Englishman, and he at once lent us one, when, to our horror, the news arrived that the Boers in charge of the oxen had taken away the team and left the waggon in a rut, all to one side, and there it had to remain all night. A few of us put up at the canteen, a small clay shanty. We fortunately managed to procure some tinned provisions, and after a frugal meal, some on the floor and some in the passage, all managed to sleep in a way. The first thing next morning was to try and get the coach out of the rut, and we had to tackle the surly Boer, and for £10 he promised to take the coach into Fauresmith. Some walked in, but four of us remained to negotiate, and of course the unfortunate lady and child, who had been in the coach all night, as it would have been quite impossible for her to have waded through the sea of mud to the canteen, and, doubtless, she was more comfortable where she was. At 6 p.m. we reached Fauresmith, and met a yoke of oxen coming to tow us in. The track was in such an awful state, that although in the morning and afternoon a coach started to meet us, they stuck outside, so no relief could reach us. I thoroughly enjoyed the night's rest at the hotel, not having been in bed for four nights, and it is hard work pushing the coach and walking through the mire.

We were off at 7 a.m. on the 10th; very bad going at starting, as, owing to the late rain and the nightly frost, the usual ruts had been frozen hard, and the sun had just melted the top, so it was very greasy, and how the horses kept their legs I don't know. Met an amusing man last night at dinner. He said, "If you travel in Africa you must make up your mind to 'all *comforts* those who enter here abandon,'" parodying the well-known inscription of Dante's over the entrance to the "Inferno." I do not think he is far wrong.

Near Fauresmith we are close to the latest thing in mines—Jagersfontein (Hunter's Well). Forty-nine new claims could last year have been worked for a royalty of ten shillings; now, owing to diamonds having been found, each claim is worth £6,000, so of course there is a new rush and great excitement. Though we left at 7 a.m., we had nothing to eat till 6 p.m., when we reached Coffee Fontein. Fontein is a favourite ending of words now, as water is the great *sine quâ non* of any town, and a mining one in particular. There are two or three houses in process of building, there being a rumour that diamonds are here, and a new lot of pumping machinery is in course of erection; doubtless a few years hence this will be a city. Our horses were so done up that we could not go any further, so slept on the floor of a brand-new hotel, filthy as it was, and slept well, marvellous to relate. Off at 6 a.m., and crossed a large river, having to go down about a hundred feet to get to the bed, jolting awful; reached a corrugated shanty, where we had breakfast; on to Jacobsdal, where we outspanned, for two hours, the Modder, a fine large river close by, but even there few trees. On to Bissett's farm, where we stayed the night. We crossed the Modder river in bright moonlight, a very steep descent to the bed, and had to walk up stream perhaps three hundred yards, then jump out, and let the poor brutes haul the coach up the other side, at an angle of about forty-five degrees—cruelty to animals. It is marvellous why they do not construct a bridge, as sometimes waggons are delayed for four or five days on the banks. The traffic to Kimberley, a place of 30,000 inhabitants, is enormous, and a toll would, I should think, soon pay for the building; but, like railways, &c., every advance in civilisation and improvement is zealously opposed by the Dutch element in Parliament, and that is the reason why, in so many respects, the Cape lags behind the rest of the colonies—Australia for instance. We left Bissett's at 9 a.m. on the 12th, and reached Kimberley at 2 p.m., five days late, as we were due on the Tuesday; the delay was owing chiefly to the weakness and wretched condition of the cattle, but I did not regret it, as it enabled me to see African travel under all phases of discomfort.

CHAPTER VII.

KIMBERLEY.

CRAVEN CLUB, KIMBERLEY,

June 16*th*, 1881.

I must now try and give you some particulars of this most wonderful town—city of corrugated iron, it might be called; because, though two or three brick buildings are being erected, I do not think there is one finished, and I should not imagine that there was a slate in the whole of the place. The houses are nearly all of one storey, and not very substantially built; many of them, in fact the majority, have only mud floors, wood being so expensive, as it all comes from America. There are no forests near; in fact, the surroundings of Kimberley are barren in the extreme. Then the cartage is so great; to give you some idea, you pay 2s. 6d. for a pint of beer, and some one was telling me it was not so expensive, as the freight from Cape Town to here is 30s. per 100lbs.; now, as a box of 12 pints weighs roughly 30 lbs., you will see the freight is nearly 11d. a pint. Then there is the cost of coming from England to the colony, and the risk of breakage, so the sum total is not so surprising after all. You can imagine, from this calculation, the great expense of procuring boards for flooring houses, &c.

They are making bricks here from the reef out of the mine, and have got a machine; the bricks look rough, but they charge £12 per thousand, at one time £14; the cost in England being only 30s. or so, it is no wonder that brick buildings are the exception, not the rule. The streets are wide, and paved far better than Cape Town, and water is soon to be carried to all the houses, as a company has been started to bring it from a river twenty-five miles off; in fact, they are at work now. At present you pay so much a barrel, 3s.; in summer it is as much as 10s., and sometimes it is not to be had. This is certainly a go-ahead place. Why in Cape Town, with such a natural reservoir as Table Mountain, there is no system of a permanent supply of water? indeed, so scarce is it in summer, that I was told in the hotels there it is only safe to take a bath on the Monday, as the same water does duty all the week; but this is essentially an English place, no Dutch to stop the way, and if the latter only go out at night, when it is moonlight, and do not see the use of gas; doubtless they do not wash, except it rains.

Like in all mining towns, men predominate, and a fine looking set they are, well clothed, and independent looking; no rags. All colonials appear to be the same in build, tall and slender, and loosely put together. "Cornstalks," Africanders might be called, just as much as Australians; no rosy cheeks, but a bronzed white colour, if there is such a thing—pasty you cannot call them, as they all look healthy enough. Kaffirs, the lowest class of labour, are now receiving from 30s. to 40s. a-week, perfectly unskilled labour; capenters 20s. to 25s. a-day, and masons as much as 30s., as there is a great demand for them, owing to the *furore* about brick-buildings. Living is expensive; not exactly food, because 12s. a-day is usually charged at the hotels—cheap enough—but rent, clothes, &c. A young Scotchman came out here in the coach as a shopman to a grocer; he receives £240 a-year; and a youngster who has gone into a solicitor's office tells me he receives £360 a-year—not bad, as he remarks. Why, in London he would have been getting about £60 at the outside.

I was dining out with a friend on Monday; he takes all his meals at a boarding-house; but four have taken a house, where they sleep and have one sitting-room; they pay a white man, who looks after their rooms and cleans them, £120 a-year; no cooking of any description. Barristers here, as elsewhere in the colony, are reputed to be doing a rattling business, making their £3,000 a year or so. The climate in winter is truly delicious; nights and early mornings very cold, but days delightful, so dry and bright.

The great sight here in the morning is the market-square, where you see, perhaps, fifty waggons, with teams of sixteen oxen, loaded with all kinds of merchandise; everything is brought here, even forage for the horses. This place was only started ten years ago, and now it has decidedly gone a-head in activity, and imports more goods than any other town in the colony; including natives, there are over 30,000 inhabitants. The export of diamonds has averaged £3,000,000 for the last ten years, and there is more machinery here than in any other town; and taking the imports the same as the exports, you can imagine the enormous bullock trains there must be going to and fro, and how great need there is for a railway.

I am assured there is no fear of the diamonds giving out for years; anyhow, new mines are always being discovered, and Kimberley is the natural centre for the whole district. Before the discovery of diamonds, this part of the country belonged to the Orange Free State, but on the finding of the precious stone it was annexed at once to the Cape Colony by a Liberal Government (save the mark), and it was Lord Carnarvon who afterwards paid £90,000 to the Orange Free State, as compensation. A gentleman was telling me that he had always wondered why no Conservative had brought up this transaction in the House when there was such a row about the Transvaal. I do not blame the Liberal Government, because it has indirectly been the saving of the colony and Natal. When the mine was first discovered, and before there was any machinery, numbers of farmers came from Natal and other places, and regularly dug for diamonds, and, as many did, having made their pile of £2,000 or £3,000, returned to their farms and paid off their mortgages. Then the trade which has been added to the Colony! People are always coming and going, make some money, go home to spend it, then back again. One gentleman told me it was most amusing in London meeting so many Kimberleyites; in one hotel he once found nineteen. The speculation is enormous, and many lose, but those who win spend money freely, and after six months' in England, miss the excitement, and return; and you see that there is plenty of it; people rushing about, a new vein reported to be discovered every day, and shares jumping up and down like skyrockets. As in every other investment, if you go in for diamond companies, you must make a study of the market, and watch and note carefully the up-and-down motion; however, as I am going down the mine to-day, I shall say no more at present.

Coursing has been going on this week, but I have not been to see it, as it is held eight miles off, and people are loth to hire out horses, as galloping about takes so much out of them. They do not go after hares, but bucks, which go a great pace, and thoroughly try the stamina and pace of the greyhound. Racing, riding, &c., all flourish here, as is always the case where Englishmen do congregate. Mr. R—, who was a passenger on the "Kinfauns Castle," put me down at this Club, where I feed, read the papers, and meet people. I really do not know what I should have done without him, as 'on Sunday, when I arrived, all the hotels of any pretensions were crowded, not even a decent shake-down. I was in despair, when a young man who was talking to Mr. R—, said, "I have a room from a certain Mrs. H—, who lets bedrooms at £1 a-week." I fortunately secured one. He said, "She is a bit of a tyrant, and has an awful temper, but take no notice of her storming; the beds are clean." Mrs. H— is certainly an alarming creature to look at, of the defiant virago type of female; square built, arms akimbo, a voice shrill, face burning red, corkscrew curls, and a great talker. Before I could say a word, "A week's notice; there is no water; I do not clean your boots; one candle a-week," all vollied out at me. I gave notice at once, as I mean to leave on Monday next. I am not to be late in; hopes I am early at nights; cannot stand late hours; the keys are kept in her sitting-room, for you must know, my room is in a row of iron huts—shanties, one might call them. No chair, ceiling of canvas, with numerous holes, floor of mud, and, as the walls are of canvas, I hear every word that is said in the other rooms. The window does not fit, and I have to stick a piece of wood in to keep it open; and as to the door, it is a work of art and time to get in, but when I am once in, I do not lock it, although the door opens on the main road. This is not a very pleasing description, yet a bed is a bed. The young man kindly gave me half of his jug of water the first night; since that we have had a supply, and I have also procured a chair, and there is a bathing establishment close at hand, where I can get a bath and my boots cleaned; so "All's well that ends well."

I went to church on Sunday; an iron building of large size, cruciform in shape. All clergymen high here, high altar, &c., and being Trinity Sunday, they had flaming red copes. A good choir of men, for boys have all been turned off, owing to misbehaviour. A new organ has just been erected, but it is not to be used until con-

THE MINE. 69

secrated by the Bishop of Bloemfontein ; it cost £600 in England, and the carriage up here from Port Elizabeth and freight from home, £1,000. Freight is certainly an item out here. A very crowded congregation.

Yesterday I descended the great hole that makes Kimberley what it is, or rather the cause of there being any Kimberley at all. Mr. G—, who has taken down Trollope, Froude, Sir Bartle Frere, and all other notabilities, very kindly acted as my guide. He has to do with far and away the largest claim here—the Central—now a large company ; in fact, nearly half the mine belongs to them. The hole is difficult to describe, so to give you an idea, I may say it is a deep, artificial hollow, three-quarters of a mile in circumference, and over 300 feet deep, all dug out since 1871, and partitioned off into various claims. If, as they say, the Kimberley mine is to become the property of one company, half the attractiveness of it will be lost, at any rate from the spectators' point of view, for the numerous claims will all be rolled into one, and the subdivisions and partition walls will be done away with. At present the bottom of the mine resembles a Pompeii unearthed at a depth of three hundred feet, with its square upstanding blocks of roofless houses, with this difference, that instead of the glaring white walls, all is of the prevailing blue colour, and instead of its resembling a city of the dead, the Kimberley Pompeii is all alive with thousands of Kaffirs, swarming like bees, digging and shovelling; and what with the whirl of the machinery and the continued hum of the human hive, it resembles a species of Pandemonium. The blue soil is where the diamonds are found, but after exposure to the air the blue turns to white; there are numberless veins of other tints, red, yellow, &c., and it is this diversity in the colouring of the reef that gives such a picturesque appearance to the whole scene by day, and by moonlight makes it look so strange and weird. In the indistinct light, one gains an impression, though perhaps exaggerated, of the immensity of the undertaking, as the pit seems nearly doubled in size and of an unknown depth. It is certainly the most wonderful sight of the kind in the world, and is probably a unique example of what man will do to enable him to make money; and a more money-producing three-quarters of a mile than this pit has never before been heard of, or even read of in the "Arabian Nights."

How diamonds were first found here, and the general rise of the place, is to be got from guide books, so I will not go into the whole history; and doubtless all of you will have read Trollope.

In the year 1867 a man noticed a Dutch child using a remarkable looking stone as a plaything; he found on inspection that it was very heavy; the mother presented it to him, and it was sold for £500 to Sir P. Woodhouse, who had been governor of the colony; curiously enough, when I was in Bombay in 1874, I remember His Excellency showing me a huge Cape diamond off colour, that is, of a slightly yellow tinge. Then the celebrated "Star Diamond" was found in the possession of a witch doctor; it was of the purest water. It was after this date people flocked to the mines, first of all to the Vaal River, then to Du Toit's Pan, De Beer Mine, and lastly to Kimberley, which has averaged for the past ten years £1,500,000 worth of diamonds, or just half the total of all the mines, which produce about £3,000,000 worth per annum. Mr. G— remembers when the Kimberley hollow was covered with grass.

We scrambled down the sides of the mine to the Central Company's claim, and on reaching it one began to take in the reasons for the subdivisions, and how each claim was kept and worked separately, and one had some conception of the extent of the works carried on below. It certainly was a curious scene. Clambering over the wall and blocks of the reef was anything but pleasant, as, owing to the recent rains, the mine was half flooded, and the state of one's boots and clothes was a caution. We watched the process of getting out the blue. At each of the separate mining company's claims was a gang of Kaffirs at work, with one or two white overlookers. The first thing to be done is for the men with picks to loosen the blue stuff, which is very hard, in fact, it resembles rock, but crumbles away in water; blasting is now very much resorted to; the stuff is then shovelled into small waggons, which are shoved on a tramway line to the sides of the pit; the contents are tipped into large iron cylinders, which are suspended on wire ropes, or aërial tramways, as they are called, which stretch to the top of the mine; you pull a wire, and up goes the bucket at a great rate till it rests on one of the enormous wooden erections which surround the edge of the mine. The blue is then upset into large wooden boxes, and goes down a shoot into carts which are underneath. At first the stuff was pulled from the bottom of the mine by hand windlasses, next by whims, which were turned round by horses, now everything is done by machinery. The carts instantly go off about half a mile to the sorting machine; here the stuff is unloaded into a revolving sieve of large size, and all except the lumps—which are still solid and slip down another shoot, and are taken away in carts and spread in the sun to dry—goes into a centrifugal machine. This turning round rapidly (water, of course, being introduced), all mud, &c., is washed down a shoot, leaving the blue stuff, which is heaviest, at the bottom; this then goes through a still smaller sieve, is put on a table, sorted, and the precious stones, if any, picked out. They have large bleaching, or rather drying, grounds attached, and from here the stuff, when dry, is taken and washed again, and the large pieces that would not dissolve at the first attempt are now, when dry, put through the same process.

There is great loss in mining owing to the stealing of the stones by the Kaffir boys, who have eyes like hawks, and although nobody except licensed dealers have a right to buy stones, numbers of unprincipled men, chiefly Jews, with whom the place swarms, try to induce the Kaffirs to steal the diamonds; they purchase the stones from them, and try to smuggle them to Europe. If anybody is found buying a diamond from a Kaffir, the punishment is very severe—five years' penal servitude; it is quite right it should be so, for owners must be protected from the illicit traffic. There is stationed over each gang of Kaffirs in the mine a white man, who looks on to see that no diamonds are picked up; the latter is generally a youth, as his eyes are sharper. I have heard of a Kaffir who placed a stone between two of his toes, worked all day with it, and when he reached the top of the mine in the evening it was still found on him.

An engineer informed me that a twelve-foot machine will wash 300 tons of stuff a day; on an average 30s. a ton is what may be got out, sometimes £5 a ton in value. The great expense here in using machinery is the fuel; wood is £20 a load, and coal, unprocurable, £48 a ton (a few bags were once bought up at that rate); £3 a ton at Cape Town, but the carriage is so great. There are coal mines, and a company has been formed to work them, and a railway is to be made to them.

The mine was at first divided into 816 claims, then into 416, now all the claims are bought up by large companies—far simpler. A thirty-foot square claim, which ten years ago cost almost a nominal price, if in the market now would fetch from £11,000 to £20,000. The value of the mines is put at £14,000,000 for nine acres of ground. They are now 300 feet down, but find that they can go easily to 600 feet, and the boring shows that the soil is diamondiferous to that depth. Water is now the great trouble; the reef also at the top of the mine keeps tumbling in. A steam navvy has been sent out from England, and a company formed, who undertake for £800,000 to remove the reef and make the sides of the mine at an angle of forty-five in two years. Two engines take the trucks with the reef outside the town; it was the first time an engine had been seen here, and the excitement was intense. Kaffirs were in the seventh heaven, and one unwary chap had his head cut off, falling down before it. Two of the largest companies—the Central and the French—have tunnels from their claims, 400 feet long; the waggons run along them with the stuff, and are hoisted up to the surface direct, which saves the wire-rope business, and is simpler.

The days for picking up diamonds are all gone. A young fellow told me that when he came out, eight or nine years ago, to Du Toit's Pan, he met a man who said he must have gold, or else his Kaffirs would strike—he wanted £9 to pay the wages—so he gave him in exchange for the money a diamond which the young fellow sold for £50; it was afterwards bought for £150. At the first rush officers in the army, barristers, and in fact half the world, flocked here; but when diamonds were no longer found on the surface, those having no capital went to the wall, and hence the companies. The Mining Board keeps the mine clear of water and reef, or is supposed to do so. Mr. G — told me they pay £5,000 a month as rates; the whole mine is rated roughly at £200,000 annually, so they can afford some improvements. They tried to start a Gladstone Company, but could not float it;

people were too patriotic even to make money under such a name, so its designation had to be changed.

It certainly is a wonderful sight to look down and see the three thousand men or so at work. They resemble variegated ants, owing to the colours of their shirts; and to see them coming from their work along the narrow paths looks like a moving column of the same sagacious little animals. The hundreds of wire ropes leading from the various claims to the top of the mine appear like spiders' webs, and the tubs coming up do well enough for the spiders—all similes in the animal line. The origin of the diamondiferous soil nobody appears able even to conjecture.

There has been a great deal of money made this spring, but shares are down again: the Centrals, which are now at £400, started at £100 paid; last year they distributed 92 per cent, which at present price would give about 23 per cent.—good enough, and very good for the original shareholders. They generally calculate in the year of taking £300,000 worth of diamonds, and I am told on good authority that mining is likely to pay if they can do away with illicit diamond dealing, and if as they get deeper they can keep the water down. How money is made is by buying shares in claims only just worked, or resuscitating those that have been abandoned—as, for instance, Jagersfontein, where shares which last year were only at £25 are now at £225; but it is regular gambling. The number of brokers is surprising—whole streets of them. I went to-day to see Du Toit's Pan, but it is useless to describe it, as it is so like the Kimberley mine, although no individual hole is so large.

There is every variety of race here, Kaffirs, Basutos, Hottentots, Malays, Chinamen, white people of every nationality, and numbers of doubtful parentage. Saw a Kaffir fight yesterday; like all native combats, the palaver lasted half an hour and the fight about ten minutes; they fought with fists, and to see the gesticulations of the crowd was very amusing. They seem, as a rule, quiet, inoffensive races, and supremely happy, as they ought to be with £2 a week wages, and as I suppose they live on 5s., they save money, and then return to their various tribes. Now the Basuto War is settled, numbers of the native Basutos will come here. They are a loyal race, and hate the Boers. I am told, but I do not vouch for the accuracy of the story, that in the late war with the colonial forces, if the band played "God save the Queen," the Basutos saluted, as they are and always have been proud of being directly under the Queen. They are an agricultural and industrious race, and prospered immensely under our protection. Their land is fertile, and they grew and exported wheat, being far more go-ahead than the Boers. They are a different class to the Kaffirs, Fingoes, &c., who were deprived of their arms, and rightly so, as they were always robbing and stealing. The Basutos only wanted arms for protection against the Boers, and, as it turns out, they will have them. The war has cost £1,500,000, plenty of ill blood, and without anything being gained by the Cape Colony. I heard a rather amusing story the other day, on good authority. The Dutch, ignorant as the majority are, are telling the most fabulous tales of the reverses of the English to the still more uneducated Boers, who, owing to the way in which they live on their isolated farms, have little or no education; and the story is this, that when the Queen heard of the defeat at Amajuba, she took to drink, was then thrashed by the Prince of Wales, and it ended in her Majesty fleeing to the Black Sea to get protection from, I fancy, the Sultan of Turkey. Even in this Club the Dutch are most insolent, always talking about the decadence of England, for they are far too uncivilised to understand any reason other than fright for giving up the Transvaal; and I heard one say the other day that England never won a fight, and asked, If England is a first-class power, what must the Boers be? If all accounts are correct, the native tribes may beat them yet, and the papers are full of the intention of loyal British and Boers, if the Transvaal is handed over unconditionally, of combining and beating the victorious Boers if they can. There is no doubt, owing to the dislike the natives have of the Boers, that the latter are in the habit of beating them to death, and Joubert himself, they say, has committed murders enough to hang a dozen people.

CHAPTER VIII.

A CURIOUS CONVEYANCE.

BLOEMFONTEIN,
June 22*nd*, 1881.

I left Kimberley in the coach on Monday at 11, and arrived here late last night; only three passengers, but quite enough, considering the wretched conveyance. If you can imagine a rickety soda water cart and three seats without backs, you can picture the so-called coach. We had to stop on the second day every hour to oil one of the axles, as, owing to some disarrangement of the wheels, it became so hot that we thought it would crack. We had an easy journey the first day, as we only drove for six hours; went through the usual amount of bumping over dry water courses and ruts. Scenery the same monotonous flat, not even varied by mountains, and treeless,

F

as the whole of the Orange Free State is. Yet we saw huge flocks of sheep and goats feeding on the dried-up herbage, which must, however, be nourishing.

We slept at a place called Boshoff, and left at 5.30 yesterday morning for this place, and had a tiring journey of seventeen hours or so, not arriving until 10.20 p.m. Very cold at starting—piercingly so, one may say—hard frost, and the sun took a long time to melt the hoar-frost on the grass. This place is the capital of the Free State, as great a contrast to Kimberley as Tarporley is to Liverpool—a sleepy-looking town. Though it is the city where the Volksrad meets, there is little or no trade, the land all around being barren, but in the season there is plenty of fruit. It is considered very healthy, the best place for consumptive patients, perhaps, in the world; it must be from the dryness of the atmosphere, not the warmth, for at 12 to-day, out of the sun, there is still hoar-frost; and though in the sun so powerful are his rays that a topé, like in India, is necessary, or a wideawake and puggeree, yet go into a side street, and the air is quite cold. What the sun must be in summer, I know not; Kimberley then is most unhealthy—fever and dysentery being rampant.

This place is celebrated for its schools; I need hardly say English are the chief ones, though in the middle of a Dutch republic. There is a cathedral and an Anglican Bishop; in fact, the college and schools are part and parcel of the whole thing, and boys come from all parts of the colony to St. Andrew's School, and many Dutch attend. The Girls' School is under the charge of the Sisters; and in taking a walk through the town, chapels with crosses on the roof are seen everywhere. There is a speech-day at St. Andrew's to-morrow, and I intend to go.

This is a city of some 3,000 inhabitants; the roads to it are shocking, and even in the middle of the town you are bumped up and down like a shuttlecock; no railway near at present, though they are going to make one in connection with the new scheme of railways in the Cape Colony; they only lately got the telegraph. I see that there are no telegraphs now in the Transvaal; it is no wonder the people are flocking out. Land worth £60,000 a short time ago cannot now find a purchaser; and that is the great hardship on the people, who, having bought land on the strength of the English government annexing the territory, find it unsaleable; what these unfortunate individuals are going to do is the question of the hour. Yesterday I called upon some people to whom I had a letter of introduction; they talked of having to go to Kimberley, although settled here for years, and in a nice house, as, since the defeat at Amajuba and the disgraceful peace, the African Bund has been founded, and it is getting so unbearable for the English people that they will have to leave. The Bund is a society started for turning the whole of the colony into one great Dutch republic. No Dutchman you meet but believes that we ceased fighting and made peace because we were afraid, and the walls of this hotel and a house we were in yesterday are adorned with pictures of the Amajuba disaster, Ingogo River, &c. They say that General Sir Evelyn Wood is the only one who is holding out for terms that were agreed upon as essential, and that Judge Villiers, who is a Dutchman, and Sir Hercules Robinson are for conceding everything.

I start on Friday for Harrismith, and shall, if

all's well, reach Newcastle about the 2nd or 3rd. This life suits me very well, and I have seen a good deal of different varieties of the human race, if not of scenery. Some of the Boers are certainly splendidly-built fellows, as well set up as English soldiers, but half a foot higher. At a Boer's farm, the other day, I saw three or four strapping youths who would have gladdened the heart of the recruiting sergeant. One cannot blame them for wishing to have a republic of their own; the way they are going to get it is where the shoe pinches.

This afternoon I strolled up a hill on one side of the town to a fort, if a building containing a few obsolete guns can be dignified by that name. The flag consisted of a small Dutch one in the corner, the remainder of large white and orange stripes; it was the flag of the Orange Free State. Appropriately enough, I saw in a garden splendid orange trees, covered with fruit, and other trees leafless. From the hill I had a fine view of a paper-chase, for the St. Andrew's boys had started two hares with the well-known bags of paper, and as one of the members of the school was *hors-de-combat*, I had a long talk with him. From the hill Bloemfontein looks well enough, with its clean-looking houses, their corrugated iron roofs shining in the sun, its broad streets with rows of gum trees, and the small river Bloem planted its whole length with willows. The principal buildings are the large Dutch Church, the Volksrads, or Houses of Parliament, the Anglican Cathedral, the Roman Catholic one, the Convent, and the large Home for Girls, the last four of dark red brick, with the usual roof. The one building in contrast to the whole is a dark red one, with neatly thatched roof and high red brick mediæval chimneys—the Anglican Bishop's palace,—and very pretty it looked. In contrast to Kimberley, this town may be called a South African Oxford, so it is right that it should have a quiet, peaceful look. In summer there is shade enough, and it must be a pleasant change from the heat and glare of Kimberley, of which it is a sanitorium, for then the river is full, and though the heat is great, the air is tempered by frequent thunderstorms.

I must try and give some account of the educational capabilities of the place. First, there is the Grey College, a Dutch institution, where all lectures are in Dutch, though they have one master

EDUCATIONAL CAPABILITIES. 87

to teach English literature. Next in importance comes St. Andrew's School, quite on English principles; then St. Cyprian's Theological College, also English; and then the Girls' Home, where over one hundred girls are educated by Anglican Sisters; a Nurses' Home is combined in this. All these are under the immediate superintendence of the Bishop. There are also a Dutch Institute, a Roman Catholic Convent (where girls are also taught), infant schools, &c. The majority of the population here are English, but out in the country nearly all the farmers are Boers. The newspapers are half English and half Dutch.

As far as I can make out, the Dutch are essentially an agricultural people, but all the banks appear to have, as in most colonies, Scotch managers and clerks; the merchants, I think, are chiefly English.

I am glad I came to Bloemfontein, as it really grows upon one, and one can potter about here very pleasantly for two or three days after the jolting of the coach. The worst of the hotels out here is, that there seem to be no single bedrooms, and my companion has to be up at 4.30 a.m. to-morrow, to start on his travels, so my sleep will be broken. I had looked forward to a good night's rest, as I am off myself on Friday at 4.30 a.m., and shall be bumping about in coaches for a week.

CHAPTER IX.

ST. ANDREW'S SCHOOL.

LADYSMITH,

June 27*th*, 1881.

I dare say you will not be much the wiser when you see the heading to this letter, but it is a town of some importance in Natal, and on the direct route to Newcastle, whither I am bound. The day before leaving Bloemfontein I went to the speech day at St. Andrew's School; there were recitations, and, as usual, the national anthem. I did not care for the Volksleid. The Bishop of Bloemfontein gave a long address, but the best was that of the Archdeacon. Manliness, geniality, and virtue, he said, were the three things that schoolboys ought to strive after, and they do comprise about all that is necessary. They were nearly all English boys. In Grey College, next door, though nominally Dutch, English is taught, and there are numbers of English there. In fact, through all the Free State Englishmen predominate in the towns, and even in the Telegraph Office the clerks are English, as anything that requires a little knowledge is too much for the Boers. They stick to the farming interest, and their coffee and tobacco—for they are a very abstemious race, and drink quantities of coffee, ten or twelve cups a day; certainly, in this respect they beat the English, and there is a saying, Never employ a Boer boy who speaks English, as he is sure to be a blackguard, having learnt all the vices and none of the good qualities of the Englishman.

We left Bloemfontein at 5.30 on the Friday morning, and had three or four pleasant passengers; one had lived all his life in the Free State, in fact he was half a Boer, so I had a good deal of information of interest about the Boers in general, Transvaal business, &c., from a different point of view. We went through the usual amount of bumping, but had no incident of note, and reached Winberg at 8 a.m. We passed through a splendid country for sheep, of which we must have seen thousands. The grass is now dead, being killed by the frost, so one cannot judge how the country looks in spring and summer.

This is the country which England gave up to the Boers about thirty years ago, because the then shrewd Governor said it would only be a useless appendage, and all it could support were a few wild deer. It is about the best grazing ground in the world, and with the diamond fields of Jagersfontein and others in the territory, coal mines, &c., it is in a fairly flourishing condition, thanks to having the Cape Colony on the south and west, and Natal to the east. All the business stores, &c., are kept by Englishmen.

I went to the Dutch Parliament at Bloemfontein, and heard a debate. They are going to make a railway to the capital from Colesberg, in the Cape Colony. The President for the time being is in the hotel, and I had a good deal of talk with the editor of the leading paper, who, need I say, is an Englishman, a neutral kind of man, as the publication is half English and half Dutch. There is no doubt that the best Boers are in the Orange Free State, and, as far as I can make out, they like the English, as they know it is the latter that keep the commerce going, and most of the men have something to lose. The discontented Boers—ignorant, prejudiced, bigoted, hating laws and education, wishing to escape taxes or any settled rule, and desiring to have magistrates who would always decide in favour of their friends—have emigrated to the Transvaal. I was assured that very few Free State Boers helped the others; in fact, many sympathised with the English, as trade was increasing so much with the Transvaal, and as the bulk had to come through their territory, it increased the value of their property. Now all will be anarchy again directly the British leave, and all business will be at an end. People are leaving by hundreds. I was told by one gentleman, a Dutchman, who lived in Pretoria, that land which had cost say £50 was unsaleable, and one man, a German, who had property bringing in £580 a-year, wanted to sell it for £3,000, and could not get a bidder. Houses sold for nothing, one may say, as if the Boers get their way again, all enterprise will cease. The loyal Boers, of whom there are numbers here, have been turned out and their homesteads burned down, they themselves barely escaping with their lives. I was talking to-day with a Mr. M —, who was shut up in Potchefstroom and besieged there. He told us that one Boer who spoke to him and showed him some kindness when he was taken prisoner, was fined £50, and next day £5. Then some of the Boers went and burnt the unfortunate man's homestead, set his crops alight, and took him out to see the remains. Numbers who were loyal have been treated the same way, and no redress; as Mr. M— said, not even thanked for risking all for their then rightful Queen. However, if the country is handed over, the loyal Englishmen and Boers are going to join the Kaffirs, who say they will drive the Boers into the sea. Whether they can do it I know not, but I thoroughly believe they will try. The Boers will probably fight amongst themselves, as there are two distinct parties now, the utterly lawless and the respectable. The former carried the day before, and may do so for a time again; they have nothing to lose; but many who are well to do liked the English rule, because it meant prosperity. However, I really cannot tell all I have heard, as it would be too lengthy, but there is one thing certain, that further bloodshed is a necessity when we move out of the Transvaal, unless the neutral territory is given up by the Boers, as it means *slavery* to the Kaffirs, and they would sooner try and exterminate the Boers than undergo that again. They will do anything for the English.

At present the Transvaal is nominally governed by England till the six months' armistice is expired. All are agreed that with a bankrupt treasury, no army, and the fear of being swallowed up by the Kaffirs, the Boers, a year later, would have asked for annexation, only the pear was plucked before it was ripe, hence all the trouble. There is so much ill blood set agoing by this late war, that an Orange Free State man told me civil war must be the result, owing to the numbers of loyal men in the Transvaal who sided with the English, but were commandeered and had to fight with the Boers, and these men having been turned out of their farms and lost all, though nearly related to the successful Boers, will join the Kaffirs and fight against them. *Time alone* will show whether all these surmises are correct. The impudence of the Boers is dreadful; they call Englishmen curs, their papers are full of the cowardice of English soldiers, there is no holding them, and it is these swaggering fellows whom Joubert and Brand can hardly manage to keep in order now. The troops are all now on the war footing, and, as you may suppose, are longing to have a cut in at the Boers. I see even in the *Fortnightly Review*, that extreme Radical organ says it thinks the arbitrament of the sword will have to be resorted to again, and the bloodshed will be frightful; however, nothing definite is known here about the commission.

The 41st regiment, part of the 21st, and the 14th Hussars are here, the latter just from India, with white horses having Arab blood in them. I am in the room of an officer of the Ordnance; he took me up to the camp yesterday; in fact, has been most civil; he introduced me to several people, and has given me letters to others at Newcastle. He pointed out to me the two rocks which, if there is another war and the Free State Boers are likely to come and assist the other ones, will be guarded, as they command the main road between the Free State and Natal.

As I mentioned above, we reached Winberg at 8 on the evening of Friday, and left at 9 for Bethlehem, travelled all night, and reached our destination at 2 in the afternoon—a long tedious journey, intensely cold, as we are now about 6,000 feet above the sea level, and rapidly ascending.

We left Bethlehem at 7 p.m., and travelled all night to Harrismith. This was the climax of African travel—an ordinary two-wheel post-cart, with no regular seats or back, and three passengers. It was a very rough cold night, blowing hard when we started. We had four horses, and we were bumped along an unusually stony road, with boulders here and there, over which we shot at a great pace. We had not time to think of much except to cling on like grim death. At about 12 the wind ceased, and a dense fog came on. We lost our way, and for four hours we were groping about in the dark in morasses and watercourses, now at an angle of 45°, and then shot into the air; at 4 a.m. we fortunately reached a farm-house, and stayed for two hours till daylight. There are numbers of rivers all through this part of Africa, and plenty of water. This is the best season to travel, as they are 50 feet higher at times in the summer, and people have to wait for days on the banks. Between Winberg and Bethlehem we stuck in a water-course in rather an agonising manner, the splint-bar giving way, but the boy waded in and patched it up in some manner, and we got out, but it was not a pleasant sensation. From the farm-house we galloped the last nineteen miles in one hour and three quarters, which was good going, and we reached Harrismith at about 10 a.m.

I have been lucky up to this time in having no bones broken, and long shall I remember last night's drive on a small post-cart through the keen night air. There was no covering to the cart, which I thought dreadful at first, but was thankful for it afterwards, as if there had been I should literally have broken my head against the roof, or have been suspended like Absalom, for though my hair is not a glory to me, yet if one reads Scripture aright, the pictures one generally sees of Absalom are wrong—he was suspended in the fork of a tree, not by his hair.

We left Harrismith at 10.30 a.m. for the Rising Sun. Since leaving Kimberley I have not been in bed for two nights, and very short hours on the previous ones; up at 3 in the morning, or thereabouts; yet I feel very well, so I suppose roughing it suits me. I have had little time for writing, much less for reading, but if all's well at Durban, I shall have a rest. Since leaving Capetown, out of twenty-eight days, I have been actually travelling for eighteen. Harrismith is a border town between the Free State and Natal. We ascended the Drakenberg mountains, and down Van Reenan's Pass into Natal. To give you a true description of the road would seem exaggerated, because nobody could conceive it unless they had actually experienced it. We had four horses in a two-wheeled vehicle, fortunately on steel springs. The road was almost perpendicular: rocks, stones, and anon water-courses abounded, and over these we went at a great pace. Two passengers were in front and three of us behind, with our legs dangling over to balance the cart; one was never still, first up and then down; it was indeed the acme of discomfort; the cushion slipped down, everything, including ourselves, banged about, and so we descended into fair Natal.

The scenery is grand and wild in the extreme on the Harrismith side. On the Natal side, in summer, what is a vast expanse of low hills, verdure clad, is now, in winter, a sea of dark red hills covered with a short kind of grass, only wanting the rain to change it into its proper colour. The clearness of the atmosphere enabled one to see an immense distance. It was worth the week's bumping to see this splendid panorama. We reached the Rising Sun at 10 p.m., after having again lost the road, which was a mere track across the vast plain. I stayed the night at the Rising Sun, and came on here, a distance of ten miles, where I met the coach for Newcastle. An old farmer, with his wife and son, who were coming to sell forage, gave me a lift in their trap for 10s. There is a fine river here, and the cavalry horses are brought down to drink at 4 o'clock. I hear now that Amajuba is twenty-five miles from Newcastle. I had always heard before that it was only eight, but, as usual, distances increase the nearer you get to a place.

CHAPTER X.

A SANGUINE WOMAN.

Ladysmith,

July 4*th*, 1881.

As they say in the play, "What! still here?" you will exclaim. I am here, but returned last night from Newcastle, having been up Amajuba and all round Lang's Nek. I had quite intended going to Rorke's Drift from Newcastle, but could not hear of horses or buggy, though it was not from want of importunity, because everybody who possessed wheels in the town was, I think, asked. I called on vague people, was shown into their houses, and one lady promised me the loan of her buggy, though her husband intended to use it to go himself to Utrecht, but she said, "Oh, he can ride." Unfortunately, he did not see it in the same light. I do not blame him, but then woman is of a sanguine temperament, and sometimes counts without her host. I then tackled a Mr. M —, as a *dernier resort*, the largest storekeeper in the town; he also was helpless. Last summer a gentleman had been in the same plight as myself, and he had managed to procure a trap; but summer is summer, and winter is winter, and horses are so poor now, owing to the badness of the grass, that they are difficult to get in a fit state to drive or ride; then the lung disease is prevalent, and the officers have taken up all available beasts, so I came back here to try my luck, and think I see my way, if I have perseverance to insist and keep hammering away; if not, I must give up seeing the scene of, alas! the only bright episode in two disastrous wars, as far as our prestige goes, and be content with having done, as Mark Twain says, "my level best."

I left here last Tuesday, two hours earlier than I expected, and I had just time to post the letter and see Major L—, when I had to start off in the coach, with one lady passenger. The scenery I will not describe; it was the same as ever, but from here to the Ingane River the road was in an atrocious condition, consisting of blocks of stone. I really think that although we reached Sunday's

River at 5, it was the hardest day I have had. We had a large number at dinner, perhaps twelve; amongst them were two 7th Hussar men, whom I knew. I heard a rather amusing story of a Colonel; he is a man who detests natives, and prides himself in not learning the Kaffir language. One day his servant came to him, asking him something, but the Colonel could not understand him. At last an officer ventured to remark, " The man says he is ill." "Ill, are you, you black beast? if you would only turn yellow, green, or any colour except remain black, one might be able to tell whether you are ill or not; but it is impossible, with that wretched skin of yours, to know whether it is true."

We left Sunday's River at daybreak, and had a peculiarly rough journey to Newcastle. We passed numerous rest camps for the wounded coming down country. I cannot conceive how they can survive the journey. We also passed various stations for troops, and forts are being erected at Biggarsberg and other high peaks, to prevent inroads of the Boers for the future. This precaution is rather late in the day.

Newcastle is a wretched-looking tin-pot place.

Fort Amiel, where the troops are, is on the opposite side of the river, and lies in a healthy situation on a high cliff. The river is now fordable, but in summer has to be crossed on pontoons or by boat, and is dangerous at times. At the back of the hotel is a swamp, and bottles and rubbish are thrown about anywhere. There is no municipality or sanitary arrangement; no wonder, therefore, it is unhealthy in the summer; but in winter it is right enough. A mushroom kind of town, filled with loafers of all sorts, the usual followers of an army, for we have more than 14,000 troops, one way or another, in Natal and the Transvaal.

I at last managed, late at night, to engage a white pony, with high character, to take me to Amajuba. When I saw the beast in the morning, I was glad that our Secretary to the Society for the Prevention of Cruelty to Animals was not present. The framework was there, but little else— an unkempt, unshod pony, about fourteen-two, with a huge saddle, and a blanket to keep the latter off the backbone. I started in surprise at the apparition. Twenty-one miles on this animal appeared impossible, yet I did it; but it was harder work for the rider than the pony, for, marvellous to relate, it stumbled not; it crossed rivers, over slippery rocks, and we did fourteen miles in three hours. I then put him up at the hotel, near an historical spot—the Ingogo river. *En route* we passed Signal Hill and other stations for troops, and I had quite an interesting ride, all the names of places being familiar, and right in front one saw a high square table mountain, which one knew to be the notorious Amajuba.

In mentioning Ingogo, you will doubtless recognise the name. It is here, when Sir George Colley was encamped near Amajuba, that he had his communications interrupted between his camp and Newcastle. He sent the 58th Regiment to open them up; they were met here by the Boers, and a sanguinary engagement ensued. It was a drawn battle, and the 58th managed to save the guns, but that was all. My informant about this battle was the owner of the hotel, who watched the whole of the engagement. It was Sir George Colley's greatest success.

Now, the difficulty of saying anything about the war, up in these regions, is the fact that Sir George was the central figure, and as the man is dead, one naturally feels chary of saying anything against him—" de mortuis nil nisi bonum "—so I shall, of course, only speak of him in his rôle as general, and not one good word in his military capacity does one hear of him from men or officers. He was brave, but his whole movements appear to have been wrong, and he thought everybody meant to do him; hence the intelligence department was useless, as he would not believe what they said; he took no advice, and was awfully jealous; he had been told of the Boers being at Ingogo, but did not believe it. This engagement was a great mistake. The Boers occupied our position, so in reality were victors, and if they had liked might have overrun all Natal, but they only went as far as the Biggarsberg and back to Lang's Nek. The reinforcements had not come up at all, and the whole country was open to the enemy. This was his first great blunder. The next was his disastrous attack on Lang's Nek against overwhelming numbers; and the third was Amajuba. From Ingogo I rode right on to Major B—'s camp at Amajuba. I had a letter to him from Major L—; he very kindly said he would put me up in a tent, and send me round Lang's Nek, &c., in the morning.

The Major is head of the Mounted Infantry—a new force meant to compete with the Boers, because, in reality, the latter are mounted infantry. They jump off their ponies, which are trained to stand still, fire, jump on, and gallop off to another point. There are 260 men and 10 officers, and fine-looking fellows they are. I made rather a mistake at first; the Major was showing me the camp,—which is pitched on the slopes of Amajuba,—horses, &c., and at last asked me to go into the large tent; the ground had been hollowed out, the walls of unburnt bricks at the entrance were about three feet high, and over them the tent was stretched, with a big fireplace at the end. I said, " Oh, the kitchen." What was my horror when I found out that it was their mess-tent; papers and pictures plastered on the low mud walls. I was silent. They certainly have not much luxury here; a wooden table on boxes, one or two chairs without backs, the majority sitting on wooden cases; tin plates, no glass or crockery; all ready for marching. Been here two months, and including bedding, luggage, and everything, each officer only allowed 50lbs.—not much. A very nice set of fellows, most kind and hospitable. I had a long talk with one who thought hunting in Cheshire the best in England. It blew hard and cold all night, fearful gusts, and I was up many times to fasten the tent-flap; no sheets, but a kind of flannel sack that I got into on a stretcher, and a shirt and a pair of breeches for a pillow; such are the accessories of the so-called pampered soldier. I naturally received a great deal of information about the fighting. What distressed Major B— was, that here, within sight of Lang's Nek, he was not allowed to occupy the Queen's territory. This he thought, and rightly too, was the most humiliating thing in the whole treaty. You will all remember what Lord Cairns said on this point in his great speech last spring. Major B— was at the signing of the treaty, and the domineering manner of the Boers, and the meek way in which we gave up everything, was galling in the extreme. Let us have tried to beat them, and then restored their territory: but what's the use of talking of the degradation, as he and all right-thinking people say, if Mr. Gladstone had settled with the Boers in August, 1880, before fighting, well and good; or even hinted at the restoration of the Transvaal in the Queen's Speech, people would have seen it was his policy, and nobody could have blamed him, but to have done it *after* the fighting—our prestige gone—was the blunder; however, we shall rue it some day.

I started on a capital pony, lent me by the Major, and the Sergeant of the 58th, who was at the first battle at Lang's Nek and at Ingogo, as my attendant guide—a very intelligent man. We first saw the hill where Brownlow made his celebrated charge with his scratch handful of men, gallant but futile. Also where the 58th made their charge, and were nearly all killed. Lang's Nek is a huge expanse of low hills, very steep, and the extent of the Boer's lines was enormous; they had thousands to our hundreds, but it is all of the same piece; the General was in too great a hurry. It is quite certain that there is no use in sending reinforcements if they are to be killed in detail without waiting for the bulk of them to come up. The men naturally got disheartened, and lost faith to a certain extent in Sir George Colley. General Wood was sent to Maritzberg before the next engagement. I have heard two gentlemen, who saw Sir Evelyn on his way up after hearing of the disaster at Amajuba, say that he was dreadfully put out at Sir George going up the hill without waiting for his march round by Utrecht to take the Boers in the rear; in fact, he said, "Sir George Colley told me distinctly he would not move without communicating with me." Why Sir George Colley did not wait nobody will ever know. He was burning to retrieve his two defeats, I suppose. The idea of seizing the hill was a very brilliant one, and well conceived if he had waited for the other troops to come up, but as it was there was absolutely nothing to prevent the Boers going—if even Sir George Colley had retained possession of the hill—to Natal, and meeting the reinforcements in detail, or marching into the Transvaal and massacring the garrisons. He had no troops to support him, or to keep his communications open, and when he was on the top of Amajuba, nobody knew what he was going to do. The Boers' lines at Lang's Nek were 3,000 to 4,000 yards distant, so unless Sir George Colley had been enabled to get cannon or mortars up the hill—which we know he was not, as the Gatling gun of the Naval Brigade had been left behind—he could have done no harm to them; though with telescopes he could have watched their movements. He may have thought that the very fact of his being up there would have scared the Boers. It did so to a certain extent, if we are to believe Aylward, whom, as I mentioned above, we met at Phillippolis. He was in the Boer lines at Lang's Nek at the time, and says that when Sir George Colley was seen on the top of Amajuba, the inclination of the Boers was to skedaddle, but Schmidt, who was in command, rallied his wavering men by saying, "You have always longed to meet the enemy; there they are; now's your chance!" and on they went. The result we all know. Only 275 men actually charged the hill. The Boers say they do not care for the infantry at all, as, from all the damage they do, they might as well be armed with popguns; and as only two Boers, at the outside, were killed at the attack on the Amajuba, they have some reason for the contempt in which they hold the line regiments. I rode to the foot of the steep part of the side that the Boers came up, and from there walked to the summit, a stiffish climb of twenty minutes or so. The English came up on the other side, a much longer and more difficult route. This side was chosen to prevent them from being seen from the Boer lines.

It is perhaps a good hour's climb, but it was night time, and the men were encumbered with their rifles and accoutrements. The hill-sides are composed of numerous ravines, thick brushwood, and huge boulders, which, on a dark night, must have been most trying and exhausting to surmount; and that is how the men were so done up when they reached the summit, being more fit to go to sleep than to fight, and then there was no food nor anything for them to partake of.

Some people think that Sir George Colley, having made no arrangements of any kind, meant to go down in the afternoon to his undefended camp, but all this, including his real object for going up, is a mere matter of conjecture. The top of the hill is saucer-shaped, and I should have thought that nature had provided natural ramparts; but it is of large extent, and for the tired troops to attempt to defend it against the Boers was too great a task. A private told me that the officers were shouting at the wrong men; and here comes another of the blunders. If there had been one regiment, or two whole regiments, it would have been better, as "Tommy Atkins" likes and obeys the officers he knows, but not those he does not know; and on that dreadful night all the various drafts appear to have been mixed up in inextricable confusion; first one gave way, and then another, and, as a sailor is reported to have said, " We took the whole night to get up the hill, but we came down in three strides." Lieut. H —, who is at Mount Prospect, and others, begged and entreated the General to give the order to charge, but he appeared to be dazed, and said to everything, "Not yet, not yet." One can only add, " Quem Deus vult perděre, prius dementat." The idea of the majority of officers is, that a charge of cold steel would have done the job, and the men would have liked it—anything better than total inaction and watching their comrades falling by their side, and not seeing the men who were shooting at them, as they were hidden by boulders, &c.

There is no doubt that the men ran away at last, and though the Boers were then only fifty yards off, numbers of the rifles picked up were found sighted for four hundred yards. This is chiefly due to the wretched system of short service, young fellows being drafted into regiments at home to fill up vacancies abroad, they perhaps not having even fired off the yearly regulation number of one hundred ball cartridges, as probably they had only been enlisted for six months. How can they be expected to fight against, perhaps, the finest shots in the world and not lose their heads. It certainly was a wonderful charge of the Boers. When one sees the hill and its steep sides, one cannot help admiring them, though indeed sorry for the result. If our troops had retained their position, I fancy the Boers would have surrounded the hill and starved them out. Sir George Colley was great at Kriegspiel, and he used to think he could move men in real warfare like he did on a chess-board. One thing about Sir Garnet Wolesley is, that he always arranged for any contingency that might happen, and never left anything to chance. Poor Sir George Colley, one cannot afford to be beaten three times so signally; one cannot help feeling glad that he met with a soldier's death.

The hill sides are now black, the grass having been burnt, and also over the whole of the top, so one may say the blackened summit is a fitting monument of one of England's worst defeats. There is a white stone cross, which stands out in

H

almost too dazzling relief to the sombre surroundings, erected to the memory of Lieutenant Maude, only son of Viscount Hawarden. "For Queen and country, Jesu mercy," is written on the one side, and on the other a long description of various regiments he served in, for he had left the army and volunteered. The view from the top is magnificent, and you see the Transvaal, Orange Free State, and Natal, and a vast panorama of hills, valleys, and rivers. It was a lovely day. I came down the side the troops came up; the ponies were at the bottom, and I rode to the camp, as Major L— said, "I'll give you a letter to Major B—, and see Amajuba, only do not talk about it." There is no doubt that our soldiers fought at a disadvantage with the Boers, because their mode of fighting may decidedly be called a guerilla warfare. They are not regularly trained, dressed, or drilled according to our ideas; each fights to a certain extent independent of the other, and are not under regular command, but their training for this kind of warfare is the best in the world; from early childhood they are taught the use of the rifle, and live, one may say, in the open air and in the saddle. They have plenty of practice at buck shooting, which teaches them to judge distances; they also know the country, and how to take advantage of every shelter that nature affords.

Sir George Colley, in his two first defeats, had hardly any cavalry at the very hour they were wanted, and instead of hurling our unfortunate infantry at the Boers, scattered behind boulders, with their ponies standing by, if he had only waited for cavalry and more artillery, he might have done something; hence arose the idea of forming the mounted infantry, as with such troops he could have coped with the Boers on equal terms; but they came too late in the day. However, we learn by experience; we must not, therefore, wholly condemn our soldiers, because they were fighting against overwhelming numbers, and against a system of warfare utterly opposed to our European ideas. If you talk to the colonists, who, like most colonists, talk big, you would think they would soon have swept the Boers away; and they speak most disparagingly of the British soldier; still what a fright they were in when they heard that the regiments were going to be recalled. No doubt their mode of living and early training is more similar to that of the Boers, so there may be something in what they say.

Major B— had gone out shooting, and after lunch I left for the Ingogo, where I stopped the night, and next morning rode early into Newcastle, and tried to arrange about Rorke's Drift, with the result you know of. I saw the Potschefstroom garrison returning into Natal. It was a pretty sight to see them winding round the various hills. There were two cavalry regiments, and as an advance guard, Lady Florence Dixie, accompanied by two officers and dogs. She is small and wiry looking, just the kind of woman to go through all the campaigning she has done. I happened to ride to the Ingogo with an officer of the Intelligence Department, coming from Potschefstroom. He says the Boers are already getting discontented. There are three sets of them, one set who want to go back to the old *régime* before the annexation—no taxes, no laws; the other—as they were in the primitive ages; and the advance party. This Boer told him that already he felt his pocket touched, as mealies that used to fetch, say, 20s., now brought only 12s. No wonder people are still flocking out, as there will be no safety in the future for property. The Commission is likely to remain for some time in Pretoria. As to the Kaffirs, they are determined to fight.

I heard rather a good story about one of them. This man was talking about the sun never setting over England's possessions, and at last, after hearing of them all, the Kaffir said, " Well, sir, Heaven can't be worth much, or England would have annexed it by now." Talking of the setting sun reminds me of Sir Garnet Wolseley's celebrated speech, in which he said that the sun would sooner change its course than that England would retire from the Transvaal. That speech did endless damage, as I have heard of numbers who bought land on the strength of his assurances, and now are ruined. England's word in these parts, for the future, will not be thought so much of. However, you will be tired of wars, &c., but the campaign that ended with Amajuba may certainly be called a " *Tragedy* of Errors."

I saw, on my way back to Newcastle, a range of mountains covered with snow. I left Newcastle by a post-cart at 4 a.m., and reached here at 8. I shall be glad to get to the region of railways again, and not have to trust to coaches or post-carts, which start at such unearthly hours, and if you miss one, you have to wait in some places a week, or, at any rate, days. Sir Hercules Robinson, on his way up to Pretoria, stayed at Amajuba; he said he had never slept in a tent in his life, so he asked for blankets. Major B— said "How many?" "Ten if you please, three for below and seven above," and when asked next morning how he had slept, he said he had felt frozen all night. He had risen at 4 a.m., and had walked about to keep his circulation going.

This is a wretched hotel, and I had to go and get a bath in the river; the water was awfully cold, but if you wait till twelve or so the sun has great power. The river is considerably lower the last week. The people are very independent. When Lord Chelmsford and the late Prince Imperial were here, they went to an hotel kept by an old Sergeant-Major. They wanted breakfast earlier than usual—7-30. The man said the breakfast hour was 8-30, and they must wait till then. He was told who they were, and he said he did not mind; if they liked to go without their breakfast, *he* did not object, but breakfast early they should not have. All meals here are in *table d'hôte* fashion.

The weather is splendid—no more rain now till August. So far as I can make out, trips can be arranged with impunity. I met an officer of the 41st, whom I had seen up country; he kindly asked me to mess last night, so I dined there; had a substantial dinner, and tasted the first champagne that I had had since leaving England— generally out here £1 a bottle—and won 7s. 6d. at cards, so altogether had a fairly successful evening. I am in luck's way, as the two gentlemen who said they thought they would go to Rorke's Drift being unable to go, I have got in with a party of eight officers, who are going to take a mule waggon and riding horses. I have procured a pony, and am going with them; they take tents, provisions, &c. We are to be away six days, so ought to have a good time. Just busy procuring blankets, &c., as there is hard frost every night.

CHAPTER XI.

A MEASURABLE DISTANCE.

PIETERMARITZBERG,

July 14*th*, 1881.

I last wrote you from Ladysmith, and here I am in the capital of Natal, where I arrived last night. I feel now within reach of civilisation again, for this is the terminus of the railway, and it is an immense relief to feel that when you want to move on you can go by train twice a day, and sure of a seat, not to speak of the freedom from bumping and jolting over the Natal roads in a post-cart. I am now only seventy miles from Durban, *ergo*, from the sea, and when I see the ocean again, I shall feel, as Mr. Gladstone would say, within a measurable distance of England.

It is six weeks since I left Cape Town, and I have had, on the whole, if not an easy time as far as comforts go, yet an enjoyable one otherwise.

I have carried out all my plans, seen a great deal of the country, have, or ought to have, a good idea of the various races, and visited places that will live in history, Amajuba, Lang's Nek, Rorke's Drift, Fugitive's Drift, up which Coghill and Melville struggled with the colours of the 24th, seen their graves, and something of Zululand and its inhabitants, and now I go to Durban, where I intend to stop ten days, cleaning up, &c., for I need it, as really, since leaving Kimberley, I have hardly been in a bed, have slept on counters, in stores, on floors, and in tents. I never felt better in my life. The weather has simply been magnificent, bright cloudless days, yet the sun always tempered by a cool breeze—the perfection of weather for travelling—and if for no other reason I cannot but have a favourable recollection of South African travel, rough as the latter is in respect to roads, feeding, and accommodation.

The scenery in Zululand is very fine, but what is now dried-up grass, is in spring a mass of living green, and leafless trees are covered with foliage; therefore it is hardly fair to condemn African scenery as wanting in fertility, and tame it cannot be called. But I had better begin by giving a short *resumé* of my trip into Zululand, though short it will be, as we only took riding horses, and of course had to take rugs and coats; so all my luggage consisted of a towel, a toothbrush, and a few handkerchiefs; writing materials all left behind. One never dreamt of wanting a change in this climate.

Owing to the transport waggons having to go to the Transvaal to bring down stores, &c., we could not get the mule waggon we anticipated, so the party, consisting of the Colonel of the 41st, three 14th Hussar officers, two Captains of the 41st, and a Captain of the 21st, fell through, the Colonel not caring to go without the tents, provisions, servants, &c.; the Hussar officers also dropped away, not caring to rough it. I went, as arranged, to stay with Captain Whitton, who put me up in his tent. I messed with him and the 41st, and very kind they all were. In the end, Captains Penno and Bewicke, of the 41st, and Captain Whitton, of the 21st, and myself agreed to ride to Rorke's Drift on ponies, with a guide, a certain Willie King, a blackleg, yet a first-rate cicerone, with a knowledge of Kaffirs and Kaffir ways, so we agreed to start on the Thursday mid-day. On Wednesday afternoon I went a ride with Bewicke to see how my nag shaped; a shapely animal he was not, white originally, now a species of black and white, never groomed, long hair, bones prominent, just had the mange badly, wounds in various parts of his body, but none under the saddle. I asked the man about him, and he warranted him. I never sat an easier animal; when he cantered he seemed quite skittish. Bewicke and I had a longish ride of two hours, and I was delighted with my mount. Had a lovely sunset; the colouring of the surrounding hills was very fine.

Ladysmith lies in a hollow; the camp of the 41st, half of the 21st, and the 14th Hussars, is in a large basin, with hills all round, and down below is the Klip River dashing and foaming over its stony bed; but there are delicious green pools of deep water, where the soldiers can always bathe; and this is the great beauty of this part of Africa, the endless rivers, now passable, but in summer you may remain for weeks before you can cross; and this is why travelling then is out of the question, and the heat is so great that it is not desirable.

We had a pleasant party at dinner; sat in our

great coats, roughing it; all on war footing; no glass or crockery, tin plates, cups, &c., and chiefly tinned meats. Colonel Winsloe, who commanded the Potschefstroom garrison, is here as Colonel of the 21st. Whitton himself saw the whole battle of Amajuba. There was also a young officer of the 60th Rifles, who had charge of the burying parties, and knew every inch of the ground. As I said at the time, when I had seen the hill, how it was not held will always remain a mystery. They say that only one Boer was shot, yet it is puzzling to think that it can be true. There is little doubt that the men fired in the air, or not at all. The only chance was to have made a charge, and the impetus of going down the hill might have swept the slope of Boers, but the order was never given; after all, it might only have been a useless waste of life, as in the end 3,000 must beat 300.

Although I had nearly as many blankets as Sir Hercules Robinson, and was warm enough bodily, my head was very cold, and in future, if I sleep under canvas, I must take to nightcaps. At 8 in the morning the thermometer was only 26°; what it was in the night I know not, but it was precious cold performing one's ablutions in the open air at 8 a.m.; it made one hop around. The officers think it a luxury to get under a roof, as, being ready to go on the march at any minute, they have only actual necessaries—50lbs., including bedding; no bedsteads. However, the great Sir Garnet Wolseley says that the man who is not ready to move for the sake of his kit, had better go home to his mother. I, with my 25lbs. of luggage, not including rugs, feel quite a swell with *two suits*, most of the officers having only one besides their uniform.

We started at 2, and had a pleasant ride of twenty-five miles to a store kept by a Mr. Brockbank, which we reached about 6. Considering that, as usual, there was no particular road, but that we crossed mealie fields, then through three or four miles of country with grass reaching up to the horses' heads, we did pretty well. The scenery was certainly an improvement on what I have seen, as there were some trees of large size, much broken ground, ranges of hills, and the usual number of spruits and rivers to cross. We had a meal of a sort—very good considering the circumstances—and then to sleep. I slept on the counter, which was rather hard, but elevated above the rats, &c., with which the store swarmed, and, as I was asked to choose, I selected the high and lofty position; the others were ranged in rows on the floor. We had, fortunately, plenty of blankets. As usual, it was bitterly cold, and we sat at dinner in great-coats, and, before turning in, we had to see that the animals were all right. I shall become quite an adept at off-saddling, knee-haltering, &c.—not grooming, for these ponies are never touched, and do not need it; if they get very bad, they are washed once a year or so with carbolic soap.

All my three companions are very pleasant fellows, and Whitton has a capital idea of how the country lies, in fact a good trekker. Penno had an animal of his own, which jacked up the last stage, and had to be left behind. Bewicke had quite the finest animal of the party, one that he bought at General Roberts' sale at Maritzberg, for the General had sent to buy horses for his campaign, which, alas! came to nothing; this horse also was very ill from change of food, and had to be dealt with carefully, but Whitton's Basuto pony and my mangy beast carried us throughout, and came home as lively as they went, *i.e.*, needed no more persuasion at the end than they did at the commencement, ate their food, rolled in the dust, and were happy. As a rule, a beast of the country is the best to take on expeditions of this kind, and not a pampered animal; but I am anticipating. The guide had hired a hairless animal, or nearly so, from a Kaffir; it belied its looks, went well, and with the unaccustomed amount of food it had, it became too lively, and took to bucking and kicking. Mr. Brockbank would not take payment for food, which was very awkward, but we persuaded him to take for the horses' provender, which is really more expensive than the human commodity.

We had a charming ride of twenty-five miles—the regular stage—through park-like scenery; it was quite refreshing to see the fine trees and the ranges of hills, with their sides barren, yet ever changing in colour; the air was delicious, with a cool breeze. We did not keep to the path, but, under the guidance of Willie King, took a bee-line to Helpnakaar, which, being situated on the top of the range of the Biggarsberg, and near a gap, can be seen for miles. Through grass, in places over our heads, we wended our way, and were lucky in seeing several bucks springing into sight in the long herbage, and then becoming lost to view. Occasionally we would come to a Kaffir kraal.

Kaffir is a name given to Zulus, Basutos, &c., all alike, and is a general term for the natives. They do not appreciate it, and, like most people, even if they have no local habitation, still they are proud of belonging to some individual race. The Zulus look down on the Basutos, and these again on the natives of India, who are in Natal in numbers; but English people indiscriminately call the Blacks Kaffirs. Their kraals are not of large dimensions, perhaps twenty or thirty people in one, and three or four huts, which I described before as resembling a rounded hay-stack, with a hole on the ground for the entrance. We went to one at the first kraal, and crawled in. At first you cannot see, as the only light is from the aperture by which you come in, but at last the eye becomes accustomed to the gloom, and you can discern objects. They say they are clean, but I should be sorry to spend a night in one, as the floors are mud, and there is an absence of furniture. We had some Zulu beer, which had the merit of being cold. It is made from Kaffir oats, and as we drank it whilst in a state of fermentation, it was sourish and not very digestible. The men wear but little ; they stick a feather or something through their woolly head of hair, a snuff-box, resembling a small brass case for pens, in their ears, and feathers behind and before. This is the ordinary attire in their native wilds, but on nearing towns they must wear clothes, and this generally consists of a short shirt, or an old soldier's jacket, of which they are very fond, and the Government send out all the old coats from Pimlico. The Kaffirs like old clothing, and prefer them to new, because they argue that if a thing has been well worn, it must have been good originally to have lasted so long, regardless of the stains and patches : and when they *do* wear trousers patches are particularly prominent ; but they like their legs to be free and unconfined, so seldom wear trousers ; boots are not necessary, but occasionally they have them on. The women, in their huts, wear nothing except rows of beads round the neck, one round the waist, and garters ; but when they see Europeans approach, they throw a blanket over themselves. In the town they wear less than the men—some kind of loose robe thrown carelessly over them, more for show, I fancy, than for decency; but this being winter, I am told the covering is more ample than in the summer.

They have great woolly heads, with feathers and skewers stuck through, and often carry parasols of red, green, or yellow. These are unmistakably for show, as I have seen them, when the band of the 41st has been playing at Ladysmith, with the parasols wrapped up in paper. The women do all the hard work, and are prematurely aged, but have splendid figures and good-natured faces, and such teeth! They always seem happy and contented, forming a great contrast to the natives of India, with their placid, soft aquiline faces, and neater, yet equally graceful, figures. The latter wear the same brilliant colours, with rings through their noses and ears as in their native land.

Natal, near the coast, is semi-tropical, and close to Durban sugar is grown; the chief cultivators are the coolies; up country the latter are the cooks. The Kaffirs have to pay the hut tax—£3 for the first, £2 for the second, and £1 each for the others. Since the Zulu War the number of huts allowed in a kraal is limited ; the object is to prevent any very great number of natives from congregating together; in fact, not to allow a location to grow to the size of Ulundi, the idea of the Government being, that it will be easier to manage the country if the people are divided up into small numbers. They are allowed a certain amount of land near the kraals free, to feed their herds and flocks, and fowls abound, though they seldom eat eggs or chickens, but sell them to the white man. They all seem a happy and contented lot, and are fairly clean.

We had a steep ascent to Helpnakaar of about two miles. The rocks became quite basaltic in appearance on nearing the summit, and the rifts or ravines being covered with dark trees, made the whole look very picturesque, the grey rock standing out in bold relief against the green foliage—evergreens, I fancy, they must have been, for few trees have any leaves on at present. Helpnakaar is on a plateau, and consists of two or three houses. By the graves scattered about we know that we are nearing the seat of war, in fact, we are now only fourteen miles from Rorke's Drift. There is a hastily-constructed fort, which was erected to prevent the Zulus going into Natal, but, like all laagers and forts in these parts, a more unfortunate position could hardly have been chosen. This one in particular is in a hollow, and commanded by hills at the back and at the sides, round or down which the Zulus might have come like wolves on the fold. I of course, practically, know nothing about such things, but I have heard it universally expressed and confirmed that the majority of laagers, &c., built in the unfortunate Zulu war *after* the disaster at Isandhlana, when everything was done in hot haste, were placed in the worst positions that could have been selected. They say that General Crealock, after the great disaster, used to march four miles, and then laager; certainly one sees laagers enough to warrant the assertion. But after the first shock, as history shows, the English officers became bolder, and dashed in and beat the Zulus. There is no hotel at Helpnakaar, but a store where we put up A store in Africa is a shop, where they sell everything from a buggy to a pair of stockings, and are chiefly patronised in this part of Africa by natives, who buy blankets, old soldiers' coats, &c. We had luncheon on tinned meats; what one would do without these things, I know not. I am told, on unimpeachable authority—that of the wife of the missionary at Rorke's Drift—that the tinned meats found on the plains of Isandhlana a year and a half after the massacre were quite good. This is an advertisement if you like.

We had shake-downs in a sitting-room, I on the sofa, the rest on the floor; they had decidedly the best of the bargain, as the sofa was one of those twisty affairs that, whichever way you lie, seems to break your back; however, we were thankful to have a roof over our heads, and on these cold nights it is necessary. We were off next morning at 7, and as the sun does not rise till 6, it was cold enough. The bill was 55s. for the five horses, and 8s. for two feeds (human), rugs, and shake-downs. Wine or beer they had none, but a little "square face," a species of gin in square bottles; whether called from the shape of the bottle, or the strength of the contents making you stand up square, I know not. Drinks here are called tots, whether a corruption of Hottentot or a totting up of accounts, also I know not. People out here ask you to have a three-cornered tot, which means, say, three glasses of sherry and a bottle of soda divided amongst the three imbibers.

When we had ridden about three miles, we reached the brow of the Biggarsberg range; below us lay Zululand, and a magnificent panorama it was. Though the mist had hardly lifted from the lower valleys and ravines, numerous ranges stood out like promontories, and immediately below us were vast plains extending for miles, with the inevitable river winding along like a silver thread. As I have mentioned before, the clearness of the atmosphere here is simply marvellous, and the horizon seems boundless; consequently everything stands out distinctly. We had such a stiff descent, and so rocky, that we had to lead the ponies for some distance; but soon remounted and trotted across the plains, with the usual grass towering over our heads, towards the Drift. What hay this grass will make if cut in time! or, at any rate, what bedding for horses! but as it cannot be eaten down by the cattle before it attains this tremendous height, it is burnt, if there are any people to fire it, so that the new grass may have a chance of cropping up. Emigration is certainly wanted here, but till things are more settled, who would care to come? For you can tell by the cattle you see that the food is nourishing. The tallest of the grass is used for thatching, and in the erection of Kaffir kraals.

At last, at 10 a.m., we reached the celebrated Rorke's Drift, the defence of which was the one bright spot in the Zulu campaign. Nothing much is left of the original defences, all being pulled down, still you can see the outline of the fort. The missionaries' buildings are *non est*, but a new church is being erected, and the gum-tree stands out like a sentinel. It would be quite superfluous for me to give a *resumé* of the attack and defence, because you all know it better than I do. If the defence had not been made, there was nothing to have prevented the victorious Zulus from going into Natal, but it checked them efficiently, or so discouraged them, that they did not care to follow up their victory at Isandhlana.

About a quarter of a mile off is the Buffalo River. Even now its two arms are of considerable depth, so one had a good idea of what the stream must be in summer. The ferry over the spot where we crossed later in the day is the one which the detachment at Rorke's Drift were supposed to defend, and it is where Chard first heard from one of Lonsdale's horse of the disaster at Isandhlana. Rorke's Drift is a ravine of that name that runs up from the Buffalo River, and as the Mission Station was situated at the very end of the Drift, it also commanded the bridle-path that leads to Helpnakaar, so doubtless its situation was chosen on account of its commanding position. I am very glad I have seen it, and the place is vividly impressed on my mind; in fact, the latter part of my trip and Kimberley have been well worth coming to Africa to see.

After wandering about for some time, we rode across the Buffalo to a store, as Mr. De Witt was at Maritzberg; we baited the horses and had some food ourselves. Curiously enough, this store is kept by a Liverpool man; it is only a canvas affair, for the Basuto tribe, who were put in this part of Zululand by the English, will not allow a permanent building, only making an exception in favour of the missionaries. At 11.30 we were off on a ten-mile ride to the field of Isandhlana. Long before reaching the place, you see the mountain from which the battle takes its name; it stands alone, and is conspicuous for miles. It is of small size, no great height, and resembles a lion couchant; it is composed of grey rock, very much worn, full of caves and holes, and presents a very ragged appearance; there is no vegetation near the summit. The camp was formed, with this hill for its background, on gradually sloping ground, and certainly was a well-selected site, easily defended, one would have thought, because the Zulus were coming in from the front, not from the rear. Of course the fatal mistake was in Colonels Pulleine and Durnford moving out in detachments; if they had done as they had been ordered, and stuck to the camp, with their rear protected by the mountain, I do not see why they could not have held it against the Zulu hordes; but they were enticed out, and we all know the result. The Zulu general, Dubulamanzi, sat on the top of a neighbouring hill and directed the affairs; his aides-de-camp were Zulu runners, who certainly, from the lie and broken state of the country, could go faster up and down the dongas than the horsemen; and on the left side were stationed the reserves; these are the men who were kept fresh, and who completed the massacre, and then ran on to Rorke's Drift. The fight at Isandhlana began between 11 and 12 a.m., and as the Zulus reached Rorke's Drift about 4 p.m., they did not lose much time, the distance being quite twelve or fourteen miles. All round here the grass is six or seven feet high, so one can well understand how the soldiers could not see the serpent-like Zulus gliding in and out of the long herbage; in fact, marching through in their accoutrements must have been hard work. We saw where Colonel Durnford fell, and numerous graves. Endless relics may be picked up, but I did not indulge. They say that Martini bullets can now be picked up at Waterloo. I did not care for any memento of such a distressing event. After spending some time there—two hours or so—and getting all particulars, through an interpreter, from a fighting Zulu, we left, and reached the store at 6 p.m. Certainly, both Amajuba and Isandhlana are natural landmarks, and the latter quite unique, with its grey summit jagged and fretted by the weather, its numerous caverns and holes giving it such a strange weird look, as we gradually lost sight of it in the waning sunlight. Fortunately it was full moon, or nearly so, so we saw the mountain in all the various phases of light, and in whatever light one sees it, few battle-fields have a fitter monument than that old lion's head looking down so calmly on the bloodstained field below. It certainly is typical of the British lion at present, who appears to be asleep—witness the last news about the Fishery Claims. I see that Lord Granville allows the American Government the sum of £15,000—not ruinous, certainly, but it is the principle. Lord Salisbury agreed with the Canadian Government that no claim could be allowed to the Yankees about the payment of money, but Lord Granville, as in the Black Sea case, was much more pliable; it is all on a par with the Transvaal business—surrender everything—and so it will go on till there is nothing more that foreign governments can conscientiously ask for, or rather care to have.

Penno and I rode to the store, and then had a ten minutes' walk to a missionary, of the name of Johnson, who very kindly put us up for the night. Mrs. Johnson received us. She is a slender, delicate-looking lady to have to rough it as she must. They had a mud-house for the dining-room, then three separate round huts, very substantially built, and in one of these was a young fellow helping Mr. Johnson. Three miles from here, there are three more missionaries, and De Witt is only two miles off. There is not a large population at present, but they have a school, with an attendance of about thirty.

In the morning at 7 we were off, in a dense fog, to the store, but had to wait till 9 before we could think of starting, and just as we did think of it, a question was asked, Where are the horses? Where? Strayed away in the fog. Here was a go! We wandered about for some time, but as I soon lost the others, I turned back to the store whilst I had an inkling of the way, deeming my nag of far less importance than myself. When the fog cleared off, about 11 or so, the animals were found quite close at hand, so we had had all the excitement for nothing. We rode first to Rorke's Drift, where Bewicke, whose horse was not well, went straight back to Helpnakaar; the rest of us rode to a kraal on the other side of the Drift, and having seen a fowl caught by Zulu children, and having made the mother promise to cook it for our lunch, we started off to walk to Coghill's and Melville's grave. Had a Zulu as our guide. When first seen he was nearly in his primitive state as regards dress, but he soon put on a check shirt, and, with a stick and bare legs, he took us a straight line over everything. He had no shoes on, and the way he avoided stones, and went at a steady pace of four miles an hour without an effort, gave us all we knew to keep up with him over the rough ground; fortunately, it was not for long, as we soon again reached a cliff overhanging the Buffalo, and suddenly Fugitive's Drift burst upon our view. It is a ravine, rapidly descending on either side to the river. It is called Fugitive's Drift, from being the ravine down which the survivors of the massacre of Isandhlana ran to try and save themselves, but the river was then at a very different height to what it is now, and numbers were drowned in attempting to cross it. The gorge through which the Buffalo runs near this point is one of the finest I have ever seen; the sides rise precipitously to the height of 300 or 400 feet, ending abruptly just before reaching the Drift. The grey stone rock, steep as it is, is covered with short dark green shrubs, while below is the river, in parts deep enough for its green waters to be sparkling in the sun, and anon foaming along over rocks and stones of immense size. One can picture to oneself, while standing near the grave, the headlong rush down the ravine on the opposite side of the river, with the Zulus sending a hail of assegais after the heavily-clothed fugitives. How people stuck on their horses, or horses on their legs, I know not, but it is certain that numbers reached the river. Melville, I think it was, lost his horse in crossing, was wounded, and the colours sank; Coghill went back for his comrade, both reached this side, and, wonderful to relate, must have struggled up nearly a quarter of a mile, for the cross is on the top of a huge boulder about that distance from the river. Here it was they turned at bay, and died fighting for Queen and country. The cross is a simple stone one, placed, as I said, on the top of the rock beside which they were killed. On one side is the same inscription as on Maude's tomb on Amajuba, "For Queen and country, Jesu, mercy," and on the other the names. There is one wreath on the monument, and by the letters "V. R.," one knows from whom it came. It is faded, and yet, on looking closely under the rosette, one noticed a ruby tinge still left, which showed that the donor must have been a Royal one, as ruby velvet is a sign of royalty. Certainly it is right and fitting that the Queen should remember the two heroes who fought their hardest to save the colours of the unfortunate 24th. The graves are at the foot of the boulder where they died. There are some flowers—a few yellow everlasting ones. A finer site could not be imagined, as, placed on this huge rock, the cross is conspicuous for a long distance, and the view, as I said before, is magnificent. Just at the back is a small cascade, its waters running down to the Buffalo. I was very glad we saw this grave, not only on account of its situation, but also for the association, and for the bold and gallant deed it is erected to commemorate. The colours were eventually picked up lower down the river.

On our way back we stood on the top of a cliff, and had a view of a gorge extending for nearly a straight mile, with the Buffalo foaming and dancing along for the whole length. It really has quite repaid one coming into Zululand to see the scenery, let alone the interest attached to it otherwise. When we reached the kraal we found the chicken ready. We had to eat it with our fingers, but very good it was. We also had beans, and these, with water—which appears particularly good over all this part of Africa—formed our repast. We had quite a galaxy of Zulu beauties watching us taking our meal. Two of them had just appeared on the scene, bringing pitchers from the well, like Rebecca of old. They had little on except three or four bands of beads. Certainly their figures are fine and upright; their countenances, if not handsome, are smiling and good-natured looking.

At 4 we bade adieu, and, thanks to bright moonlight, reached Helpnakaar at 7; dined and laid on the floor as usual. Next morning we were off early, and reached Brockbank's in good time, had a bathe in the river, and then had a number of natives, from whom we bought beads. If ever the beads arrive in England, you shall have some idea of how the natives dress themselves. I slept on the counter again, or, rather, laid down, for a cat had made it her head-quarters, and if I had not night-mare I had cat-mare. Four times the beast jumped on to me, and of course sleep was out of the question; in fact, I was afraid she would jump on my face by mistake, and I wished for daylight, which duly came, and after breakfast we trotted into Ladysmith, which we reached on Tuesday at 1.30 p.m., after a very successful trip, having seen all we intended. We were within sixteen miles of the Prince Imperial's tomb, but I had not the slightest wish to go to see it, and I do not think the others even mentioned it.

I lunched with the 41st, bade adieu, and left at five in the coach for Maritzberg, so I did not lose much time. I fortunately had engaged my seat a week before, as there was only one vacant place, and I got it. We went on till 2.30 a.m., and slept at Estcourt; it is where the Natal police have their head-quarters. We were off early, and outspanned in the middle of the day at Howick. Close at hand there are splendid waterfalls, one three hundred and fifty feet high. Even now there is a great deal of water, and it comes down like skyrockets. They are called the Umgeni Falls, and in summer numbers come to visit them, they being only fourteen miles from Maritzberg. We actually went one stage of thirteen miles in an hour and a quarter, having a good road, for a wonder. The Town Hill, before reaching Maritz-

K

berg, is four miles long, and a most tedious descent. I put up at the Plough Hotel. Bishop Colenso lives close to here. He is almost a Unitarian, they say, but Macrorie, the Bishop of Maritzberg, is a ritualist, or next to it. There is a regular split in the town, and as neither bishop will speak to each other, the congregations are called respectively " Macroricites " and " Colensoites." It is a great pity. Maritzberg is a large city, with wide streets, water running through them, and fine-looking buildings, but nothing to do for a stranger. The vegetation is rapidly changing. I actually saw a cluster of bamboos in one garden.

I left Maritzberg at 3-35 on Thursday last by train for Durban, only seventy miles, yet they take six hours; it is really only forty miles as the crow flies, but the rail descends 3,000 feet, and you twist, back, and turn in a most wonderful manner, to get down the steep gradients. There is only one tunnel on the whole line. The scenery was nothing particular, but cultivation much more general. Durban feels quite hot after the north. The thermometer the first evening was at 70°. What a change was there, my countrymen! in fact, the vegetation is semi-tropical, and though this is their cool time, it feels oppresive enough, and now, whilst writing, I feel as if I had myriads of animals running over me. I could not get a bed at the hotel, all being full, so had a shake-down in the drawing-room.

Yesterday I went to the races; there was nothing much in the way of sport, nearly every race ending in a wrangle of some sort or other, but the situation is lovely; at the back is the Berea, on whose wooded slopes the rich merchants live; below, a broad expanse of level plain, with plenty of semi-tropical forest; the green contrasting well with the brilliant hues, mostly scarlet, of the Coolie women, who were sitting about in groups. Natives of India wear here just as brilliant colours as they do in their own country. Certainly, an Eastern crowd out on a holiday does light up the surroundings; whether it would have the same effect under our leaden skies, I know not. Beyond the plain was the town of Durban, beyond that again the Bay shining in the sun, and the Bluff wooded to the top. It reminded me very much of Southampton Water, and the latter in spring is beautiful enough. You could hardly wish for a prettier *toute ensemble*.

I do wish you could see for a moment such a crowd as we saw yesterday; you would be delighted and amused. I met several officers whom I knew, one or two who were riding in Cheshire at the beginning of the year. I have had my name put down at the Club. I am enjoying the comparative rest and quiet, and have a bedroom to myself, which is *quite a wonder* in this country.

I went to a sale of ostriches this morning—twenty breeding pairs for sale. The first pair put up were called "Abraham and Sarah." "Going at eighty guineas; now then, gentlemen, how much for Abraham and Sarah?" It did sound so odd. They were not knocked down; I fancy people fought shy of Sarah. I think it was unlucky to choose such a name, for miracles are not the fashion at present. The next lot of eight averaged from one hundred and forty to one hundred and sixty guineas, and cheap at that. About ten pairs were unsold. The export of feathers is becoming a regular industry, and is increasing enormously.

Attended service yesterday; as usual, the church was called St. Cyprian's. He is the patron saint of Africa.

CHAPTER XII.

A TEMPTING OFFER.

NATAL CLUB, DURBAN,
July 27*th*, 1881.

If all's well, I leave here on Tuesday at 8 for Port Elizabeth. I go on Monday to another hotel near the place the tender starts from, or else one would have to leave so early in the morning. There are two young fellows at the hotel going to ride through Pondoland to St. John's. One of them—a Yorkshireman—is anxious for me to go, he putting me up at the end of the journey. Though I think I should enjoy the ride, there is no doubt that this is not the time of the year to see the country to advantage, so I have decided not to go.

Monday was an awful day, there being a burning wind that sent up clouds of dust and sand, for this place resembles New Brighton, insomuch that half the streets are sand. I went down to the Back Beach, from which you have a splendid sea view—such rollers and surf!—the air quite refreshing. It is the fashionable drive for the ladies in the evening. Seldom have I seen such waves.

I had a letter from Captain Whitton, in which he says that the horse which Willie King said he had hired from a Kaffir for his ride into Zululand, he had really "jumped" (the colonial expression for stolen) from a gentleman, and when he came back he sold it, though he had the impudence to write and ask for 30s. as the money he had had to pay the Kaffir for hiring the beast. How's that for high?

I do not think I mentioned that I had a very bad fall over an ant-heap near Rorke's Drift. I wonder I had not more, as the grass is so long and the ant-heaps so numerous, and near them is generally the hole of the ant-eater. I was not hurt; the pony was as much astonished as I was, and we got up staring at each other vacantly. I always went by the name of the "special correspondent," as the guide said there were three officers and a special.

On Tuesday I went by train to Mount Edgcumbe, and over a sugar mill. It is quite in the latest style—French machinery. We had a lovely ride, tops of hills crowned by the bright vivid green of the cane, which is in the process of being cut, and through at times a dense jungle, the dark green shrubs being lighted up by the various creepers twining round the branches, by convolvoli hanging in festoons, and by the crimson flower of the Kaffir boom, which, though at present leafless, is, with its silvery stem and branches, a singularly picturesque tree. Such a change, all this vegetation, after the treeless wastes of the Free State. The soil here is very fertile, but has to be cleared of jungle, and when once cleared they grow sugar. Coffee has been tried, and did well till a year or two ago, when a bug appeared and destroyed the plantations. All labour is done here by the Coolies. There are twenty thousand natives of India in Natal. In the train I met a Mr. Reynolds, who owns sugar estates, and who gave me a good deal of information. Curiously enough, he has relations in Cheshire, who I happen to know slightly.

I have described sugar crushing before, but will

give a short *resumé*. The cane grows to the height of nine or ten feet; the actual stalk is about four. The top leaves are first cut off, and then the cane is put into a shoot, from whence it goes under a steam roller that quashes out all the juice, which goes down a trough, and is carried through a series of clarifiers, subsidisers, &c., clearing the syrup of all scum and dirt. It is then led into a vacuum boiler, which exhausts all the water into steam, leaving the pure syrup. The syrup is allowed to stand in large tanks to cool. It is finally put into a centrifugal machine, which, turning rapidly round, practically converts the syrup into sugar. It is then packed off home to be refined, or exported in its present state as coarse brown sugar.

I lunched, appropriately enough, at the Saccharine Hotel, and returned to town. Certainly there is nothing equal to the green of the cane, and the crimson of the Kaffir boom would be hard to beat for brilliancy, yet there are avenues of it here. The country about, and the red soil, remind me of Singapore. The climate is very relaxing, and I feel good for nothing. What their summer must be I know not.

On Wednesday I went by early train to Pinetown, to the 7th Hussars camp, to stay with Reid. The flies in the tents were something awful, the roof of the mess-tent being nearly black. This is caused by the proximity of the horses. After lunch, Reid, Captain Phipps, and I went for a ride, I on Reid's old mare, "Kitty," which had been hunted in Cheshire this year. We had a pleasant ride over hill and dale, with lovely views, and once more one sees the ocean. Although the camp looks as if it were pitched in a healthy situation, and is high up, all the officers have had a touch of fever, but none very badly. Reid, who has plenty to do, is, amongst other things, governor of the gaol, and on Thursday morning I accompanied him on his rounds. The prison being built of sods, is decidedly the coolest place in the camp. There is nothing hotter or colder than a bell-tent, and one quite envied the prisoners their cool quarters. A number of officers of the 85th were at dinner. I afterwards played whist with Lawley and two of the 85th; I had for my partner a fierce major, who spoke not a word. Fortunately I did nothing outrageous, and I went to bed at 12. A number of the others kept it up later, and I am afraid that in trying to take short cuts some fell over tent ropes; and if there ever is an excuse for swearing, falling over tent ropes is one; it is most irritating, as they are nearly impossible to be seen on a dark night.

I slept in a spare tent, and had the usual regulation blanket bag. The weather was very hot, and unfortunately I left the flap open. About 2 o'clock or so, squalls of hurricane force set in. I awoke, thinking I was suffocating. When I had realised where I was, I began to take in the situation. The grass had been worn away, and there were inches of dust all over the camp. The tent was full of dust and bits of straw eddying about. I was nearly blinded, if one can become so in the dark. Unwilling as I was, I had to turn out to fasten the refractory flap, and was nearly twisted up by a whirlwind in a spiral column of dust. After much difficulty I fastened, as I thought, the flap, but neglected to tie the lowest rope. In the morning the servant was astonished, and so was I, to see the accumulation of dust. Talk of Friday's footsteps on the shore, there were several of mine on the floor of the tent. So thick did the sand lie, that combs, brushes, boots, and bedding were in a truly awful state. I had a bath, and felt better, but my eyes still tingled.

The bell-tent is very hot in the day, so most of the fellows have erected small square bamboo houses, with rushes for walls; very cold and pleasant they are, and you perform your ablutions in them, which is pleasanter than doing it in the open air.

When I went to breakfast I found that even old campaigners seldom remembered such a night; they had all been choked more or less. The flies are a caution; everything is placed under blue wire covers; jam is an inch thick with them. The officers just spoon the flies out, and eat the marmalade. They have all manner of contrivances to catch the animals. On Wednesday afternoon they had butterfly nets, which they drew along the roof of the mess-tent, then an officer dug a hole, and into this the flies were emptied and buried, water being scarce. Reid kindly asked me to stay, but there is a certain satisfaction of being between the sheets, and I returned to town.

I took the train to the Point, and from there hired a boat and rowed over to the Bluff; had a delicious fresh beeeze. The bar was too rough for cargo boats to cross. I afterwards went and had my usual breather at the Back Beach. The tramways are most convenient. Curiously enough, the tramcars were built by the Starbuck Company, at Birkenhead. To-day I went to the Botanical Gardens, which contain very beautiful shrubs and leaves, the lovely poinsettia being in great profusion, also palms, bamboos, &c. They are situated on the Berea, so one has a fine view of the Town, Bay, and Bluff on the one side, and the sea on the other. Had heavy rain; hope it will clear the atmosphere, or, at any rate, lay the dust, and act like oil on the troubled waters of the bar. Lieut. Morris lunched with me to-day. I had intended listening to the band of the 85th, but they did not play.

A gentleman has just arrived at the hotel from the Transvaal. He says that General Wood is looking well and hearty. The Transvaal is to be handed over on the 1st of August, and the troops are to retire to Standerton until the Volksraad sits, and formally accept what the triumvirate have provisionally. Mr. Gladstone has swallowed the leek, if all is correct; no territory is to be ceded for neutral land between the Boers and Kaffirs. This is one of the points Lord Kimberley said we were to insist upon, but as the Boers, like the Frenchmen, said "No territory to be given up," Mr. Gladstone, not being Bismarck, said "Very well." The only other question is the money one, which, as the Boers are bankrupt and cannot pay, is a minor one; probably Mr. Gladstone will give them a loan, only this would interfere with his Budget. The Government has not been right all through the Transvaal business. If it was the duty of the Government to engage in warlike operations with the Boers, it was its duty also to carry them through. If the war was unjust at the conclusion, it was unjust from the very first. This gentleman says that he went on a deputation to General Wood when he arrived at Pretoria, and the General said that if he had had any idea, when the armistice was concluded, of the state of affairs generally in the Transvaal, he certainly would not have been a party to the peace made. From all accounts he has been a fish out of water, as Judge Villiers is a Dutchman and Sir Hercules Robinson the mouthpiece of the Ministry. The officers up there aver that many of General Wood's telegrams have been suppressed. One may take this for what it is worth, but there is no doubt such an unconditional surrender could not be pleasant to a man like Sir Evelyn Wood is supposed to be. The Boers one cannot blame, as they beat the English, and cannot see why they should not have all the territory, and, instead of paying anything, receive back the £300,000 that was collected in taxes during the British occupation.

General Wood has, as soon as the Commission is over, to go to Zululand, as there are difficulties there, and also likely to be a row at St. John's, as the natives tied the Captain of a schooner trading there to the mast, and took charge of the cargo; in fact, the natives are becoming unbearable everywhere. There is little doubt that Sir Bartle Frere's policy, carried out in its entirety, was the thing—a confederation of the whole of Southern Africa, with its own Parliament, similar to those in Australia and Canada, the Imperial Government to appoint the Governors; and till that is done, there will always be fighting of some sort. The Dutchmen talk of getting up a South African Bund, which is on the same principle, but the language used would be Dutch, and of course totally free from any outside power, which would not be as good, because up to this time, although chiefs like Lerothodi, of the Basutos, and the chief of Pondoland, are willing to be under the Imperial Government, yet not under the Cape Colony; they will not care to be under anything Dutch, as they hate them so. No doubt the difficulty lies in the various races and nationalities; but in India, before the English came, there was incessant war. Now that one Power is acknowledged as paramount, order reigns. Prestige is everything with the blacks, and, as a colonist said yesterday, it would be better to fight our own battles in our own way than for the Imperial Government to fight them for us, and be beaten. The Cape Colony, for instance, carried on the Basuto War altogether independently of the Imperial Government, and have certainly made peace on terms more honourable than we did with the Boers.

CHAPTER XIII.

BLINDERS.

Fern Cottage, Port Elizabeth,
July 30*th*, 1881.

When we left Durban on the Tuesday morning at 8 o'clock, the wind was howling in an ominous manner, and on the bar "blinders" were beginning to increase, that is spray that comes against your face with the force of jets from a fountain; though, as the wind was off the land, the sea was not as high as might have been expected. There is only a rise and fall of five or six feet in the tide on this coast, so even at high water twelve feet is the limit on this sifting bar of sand. The tug we had was curiously constructed, having a single screw at each end. We had to dive below into a well of a cabin on reaching the "blinders," but it was more spray than waves. At last we reached the side of the "Danube," an old steamer—at one time belonging to the P. and O.—rolling about in a frightful manner, so bad that the companion ladder was of no avail, so they put down a wretched monkey one. Not being of that species of animal at present, though, doubtless, according to Darwin, only just removed from one, or from a worm, by a few generations, I waited for the passenger basket. I had never been in one, and only seen one once— that was in the Straits of Magellan off Sandy Point—and a very disagreeable mode of getting aboard a vessel it is. Both steamers were at times at an angle of 45 degrees, now close together, then 30 or 40 feet apart, now decks pretty level, so that you could jump on board, then down, and so the see-saw motion went on. After the ladies had gone up, it came to my turn. The basket is about 6 feet high, and they huddle three persons together. The fact of starting from the deck with one end resting on it and the other tilted up, gives one a topsy-turvy motion. At last we felt that we were swinging in mid-air, swaying in a most uncomfortable manner, then bang we went against the sides of the " Danube." We were then rapidly hoisted up over the deck of the big ship, and at a favourable moment, when the deck was comparatively level, we were deposited with a thud, and out we got. A more unpleasant sensation I never felt—a certain sinking of the lower part of the body and a swimming sensation in the head. Never go "up in a balloon, boys," never!

I knew that I was *settled* before we had weighed anchor, and I may safely say that I am unsettled now. I cannot believe in the sea doing one much good. I was perfectly well, and had been so for ten weeks on shore, and now I shall feel upset for a week or so. After rolling about, gunwale under, for two hours in the rapidly increasing swell, we weighed anchor, and came in for a regular snorter, the most severe gale that has been on the coast for years, in fact in the memory of the oldest tar—inhabitant I was going to say—nothing like it recollected. It is generally a lovely passage to East London, sailing within a few miles of the coast on a summer sea, with magnificent views of Pondoland, the Transkei, and British Kaffraria. Some unfortunate people only came on board for a pleasure trip to the Cape and back.

The First Officer began by seeing that everything was tight, extra lashings here and there, all movable fittings made as far as possible immovable, boats looked to—very suspicious, I thought. To the less experienced he cheerfully said, "Only just a precautionary measure." I fortunately had a cabin to myself. At 12 at night the rolling, the pitching, the jumping about, was terrible; the hissing of the water down the hatchway, the swishing of the water in one's cabin, the teeming rain that splashed on the deck like skyrockets—"two drops to fill a bucket," the Second Officer said; the most curious thing was the howling of the wind with all the rain, altogether making a night ever to be remembered by me. Tarpaulins over the skylights were useless, the water pouring down; in fact, when I struggled up to get a view at 7 in the morning, the deck was a miniature sea. I soon beat a retreat, as it was not safe to poke your nose outside the companion hatch without danger to the nose. During the night my old friend the carpet-bag was rolling about in the water, with shoes, boots, &c., and I had to get up to put the things in the vacant berth. Sleep was out of the question; but then I was not on the giddy mast, nor am I a sea-boy. I wished for daylight, but when it did come it was *green,* owing to the water over the dead-light being usually of that colour, so we looked ghastly enough. A few turned out, but most lay in their bunks all day. As I said, I was up at 7, but might as well have remained in my berth, as all the skylights had tarpaulins over them. The saloon was dark, a dim light here and there; the table was set, as if in mockery, for breakfast, but it was a case of shower-baths and water-proofs. Before we sat down a blanket was placed over the moist seats. We were only just keeping head to sea, making no progress.

The unfortunate First Officer was shied about the bridge by the seas, and his lower limbs were paralyzed; the Captain was simply saved by the tail of his coat. A green sea swept him off the bridge, but the return wave carried him back. Fortunately, his thick coat caught on a broken stanchion, and he had just time to clutch convulsively hold of something, and was saved as by a miracle. We heard nothing of these accidents until next day. The Captain did not lie down for forty-eight hours, and when examined on the following day by the Doctor, one side was very much injured, and all black and blue, but the First Officer being entirely disabled, he could not leave the bridge, and stuck to his duty manfully. Somebody said on Thursday, that Wednesday, the 27th of July, 1881, ought to be obliterated from the calendar. I never saw such seas in my life, though the terrific rain kept them down a bit. The "Danube" is a lively, but good, sea-boat, and no serious damage was done, though some deck-houses were smashed in as if by dynamite, and wrecked, but no lives were lost.

Thursday broke in wet, but sea moderating. At 11 a.m., as if by magic, we emerged into sunlight and calm seas, rolling about a good deal, but the change was marvellous. When, at 1 o'clock, we reached East London, we found that we had been in the tail-end of a furious gale that had sent three ships ashore, with a loss of thirty lives, and other vessels only saved by slipping their anchors and putting to sea. By the papers one learns that a storm reached Durban the night of the day we left, and there was no communication with the shore, so perhaps it is lucky we left when we did, as " All's well that ends well." Thursday afternoon was lovely, and it was only by the haggard looks of the passengers, and things strewed about over the deck to dry, that one could realise what we had gone through. The first thing that did me any good was half a glass of brandy and a quarter of a bottle of ginger-ale—a capital recipe. I then had a little soup, and gradually felt that I was myself again.

An old lady, who would insist on going in an upper berth, was pitched out, and injured her spine badly. The unfortunate husband said to me, "Never travel with an invalid lady at sea, and that lady your wife." There was a lady of enormous size on board; it took two men to get her on deck the day after the storm. Where she lay, except in the water on the floor—for all cabins were more or less flooded—I know not, for no berth could have possibly taken her in. The chair she had on deck, and all her belongings, reminded me of Gulliver's description of the furniture at one of the giant's palaces he visited.

East London has a worse bar than Durban—it is needless to say more. The only boat that rode out the gale was an old revenue cutter, now turned into an anchor boat, *i.e.*, employs her time in picking up anchors that unfortunate vessels have had to slip. This speaks for the roadstead itself. You can hardly insure vessels for East London. It was formerly the place for vessels to lie that were well insured, and that the owners wanted to get rid of. Two of the vessels that were signalled the other day to proceed to sea, did not, but let themselves drift to destruction; they are supposed to have been at the old game, but the poor fellows did not contemplate losing their lives. Out of the three crews, only four men were saved—three Kaffirs and one white man. I believe the former are grand swimmers. It is only twelve hours from East London to Port Elizabeth, where we arrived yesterday, thirty-six hours after time. I am quite convinced, as I saw in a paper the other day, that "he that cannot eat anything, dressed in any way, at any time, out of anything, under the sight of any dirt, amid any smell, and in any sort of motion, ought not to go *yotting*"— let us add, to sea; however, as I did go to sea, I ought to be thankful that we were all preserved, and that no loss of life occurred.

CHAPTER XIV.

ALGOA BAY.

Fern Cottage, Port Elizabeth,
August 4th, 1881.

Algoa Bay, on which Port Elizabeth is situated, is of large size; it is in the shape of a horse-shoe; it is not protected from the south-east wind. There are no docks, but there is no bar, and you land at a pier on which there are steam cranes and a railway; in fact, every modern improvement for landing goods, though the greater part of the cargoes are landed on the beach by means of Kaffirs, who go out into the surf and carry the various bales, &c., on their heads. They seldom drop any of them into the water, and are, physically, about the finest race on the earth, or else they could not carry the weights on their heads that they do. When I call them Kaffirs, it is not exactly right, as they belong to various nations—Zulus, Fingoes, Kaffirs, Basutos, &c. They get high wages, and work two or three months, then go back to their tribes and spend their earnings, and back again to work. The lighters, or surf-boats, have one mast, are flat-bottomed, built of wood, and coppered. When nearing the shore they turn stern on to the beach, and a rope, which is fastened from the land to a buoy some distance out, is taken on board, and they are gradually drawn in till close to the shore, and then, as mentioned before, Kaffirs go in and carry the goods to land.

Port Elizabeth is called the Liverpool of South Africa, and is a town of some 20,000 inhabitants, and is certainly a busy, thriving place; stores and business houses are all near the shore. There are some very fine buildings, notably the Town Hall and the Standard Bank. All the principal buildings are in the main street, which is of great width, and extends for a mile or so. There is not much space between the sea and a hill which rises behind, and on this hill the people live. It is a short but very steep climb, and it has to be gone up—there is no shirking it. The houses or bungalows have a particularly neat and clean appearance, nearly all being surrounded with hedges of oleanders or some other species of shrub. I have seldom seen a brighter-looking residential estate, and from its lofty situation, and copious supply of good water, it ought to be healthy. You have a lovely view of the harbour, and any breezes that there are you are sure to get.

The lighthouse is placed on a rising slope of the hill. Now, owing to recent rains, the grass is fresh and green. This piece of ground is open to the public for ever, and a monument is erected to Sir R. S. Donkin, who was Governor at one time, and after whose wife this place is called. The air is particularly pleasant after Durban, now 60 degrees, but this is their winter season. There is no smoke, and lovely clear skies, though yesterday we had very heavy rain and a gale of wind.

There is not much for a stranger to do, though, as I am staying with an uncle, I am in luck's way. Very few near expeditions. No mountain scenery like at Cape Town, or suburbs like Wynberg, but it is just the site for one of the busiest towns in Cape Colony, all having plenty to do. Next to Kimberley, it is the most enterprising town there is; and perhaps this is to be accounted for from the fact that it is essentially an English place, there being few Dutch to put their veto on improvements, and the roads are the best I have seen in the colony. The absence of trees is remarkable; except in gardens and the park, they do not appear to exist, but there is a fine stretch of country behind, where you can take splendid rides. The Club here, of which I was made a member, is considered the best in the colony, and is most comfortable.

I see by the attempted assasination of President Garfield, that heads of republican governments are as likely to be shot at as rulers of a despotic power like Russia. As the Bishop of Manchester said, in what must have been a striking sermon, "The whole world appears out of joint," and people seem not to care either for spiritual or civil law. At the bottom of it all is the increase of infidelity and atheism; if people believe in no hereafter, of course there is no fear of future punishment—nothing to deter them from committing murder, particularly when, in some cases, as in Ireland and the Transvaal, juries will not convict, though the evidence be crushing. A greater farce than the last trials was surely never perpetrated, though it is on a par with the whole dealings in the Transvaal; eight Dutchmen and one German composed the jury. Of course no evidence would make them convict the murderers of Barber, Malcolm, and Elliott. Besides this failure of justice, our soldiers who were killed in the massacre of Bronker's Spruit are unrevenged. The Boers have got everything they wanted, and the Loyalists nothing. It certainly is a premium on murder and rebellion.

On Friday I went a walk to see the Park. A year or two ago it did not exist, but owing to the new Waterworks having been opened, and there being an endless supply of water, they started one, and it is wonderful to see how trees and shrubs will grow if there is only water. The grass looks very green. I have ceased trying to explain the season for flowers in Africa. There were beds of pansies, rows of snowdrops, roses, the red hibiscus, with its dark green leaves, the poinsettia, honeysuckle, passion-flowers, Norfolk pines, &c., all within a short radius; and yet this is their winter.

On Saturday there were athletic sports, and the band of the German man-of-war played. The

"Vineta," which I visited the other day, is a training-ship for midshipmen, an old-fashioned vessel like the "Great Britain," only a thousand tons less, crowded with humans, though sixty men are ashore with dysentery. Port Elizabeth is, as you may imagine, alive with officers in full uniform; blue fever is at its height—balls, picnics, and entertainments are all the rage. I hope no broken hearts will be the result, or, what would be almost a greater calamity, any engagements, as a German midshipman's pay is not, I fancy, princely, though doubtless half of them are Counts or Herr Vons.

I hear that the officers cannot understand how the English Government allow such a parody on the Navy to appear as "H.M.S. Pinafore." It is subversive of all discipline, they declare, and turns the service into ridicule. I dare say Bismarck would stop it, but fortunately we are more enlightened as a nation.

On Sunday morning I heard the Bishop of Grahamstown preach, and in the afternoon took a stroll with G— into the country. Such wild flowers! any number of everlasting ones, in the valleys near. On Monday went by rail to the

Zwartskops River, and had a very pleasant row. After going a mile, you reach some very pretty scenery—a range of low hills wooded to the top. We landed and walked about, and returned to town about six. In the evening we all went to see "Pinafore" performed. The troupe consists of three American sisters, called Vesalius. Louise, who acted as "Josephine," has a fine soprano voice, and is decidedly fetching. Another one has a contralto, and took the part of "Buttercup;" and the third did for the sisters, and the cousins, and the aunts. Nearly all the other performers were amateurs—young men from stores, &c. It was really very well acted, and is creating quite an excitement. Almost everybody you meet is humming "Farewell, my own," or some other mournful ditty—rather late in the day to our ideas; but then Port Elizabeth is a long way from England. When will the "Mascotte" be played? perhaps three years hence.

The performance took place in the Town Hall, a remarkably fine building—in fact, I have seldom seen a finer. I hear that £3,000 has been spent on the decorations, and £6,000 more is to be spent on a clock tower, and other improvements. Under the same roof is a Free Library and Reading Room, with all the latest books, magazines and papers. On Sunday evening, at the church I went to, when the choir marched up the aisle, I thought I had seen them before; they formed part of the chorus in "Pinafore," and the tenor who sang the solo in the anthem was the Captain of H.M.S.

On Tuesday J — and I went to Uitenhage by rail, to visit a wool-washing establishment. A trap met us at the station, and we were kindly shown over by the manager. The fleeces are first put into a kind of winnowing machine, or devil, as it is called, which whirls the wool round at a great speed, and separates it; it then disappears into tanks containing very hot water, and long pronged forks, worked by machinery, are kept at work disentangling the wool; it is next put into centrifugal machines, which, moving rapidly round, squeeze all the water out, and partially dry the fleeces, which are carried out on trucks and put into large yards, spread over with white gravel, and are dried in the sun. The wool that goes in greasy and dirty comes out a dirty white; some fleeces, being of a better quality than others, are white. The boiling water is of course a necessity, or otherwise they would never get the grease out. After lunch we went over the Railway Waggon Works. I was quite astonished to see the fine machinery. All the carriages are made here, the engines repaired, and they are just erecting a large foundry, hoping soon to construct the engines. We returned to town about 6 o'clock.

On Saturday we all went to see some boat races on the Zwartkops, and we had a lovely day. G — and I had a row before the races commenced, with two charming young ladies; we tiffined at the Club House, and watched the races, which were not particularly interesting. They always take place on the 6th of August, in celebration of the day on which the Duke of Edinburgh first landed at Port Elizabeth. The anniversary is kept here as a holiday. It was a very pretty scene, the river being crowded with rowing boats and sailing craft, and though there were not the trees that one sees at Henley, still, on the opposite side of the river, there is a very fine range of table mountains, wooded to the top, and near the river a dense jungle, with masses of flowers, one of which—a pink one—very much resembles the heather at home. Then the brilliant sunshine, tempered by a fine breeze that sprung up at noon, made the day a very enjoyable one. Dancing wound up the day, and we returned by the 5-30 train to town. It is wonderful the go and energy the colonials have. There are three Club-rooms out here, where people can come and spend a day or two; everything is most complete; and when you think of the population, the young men must be actively inclined, and fine-looking fellows they are. In the evening we went again to see "Pinafore," which went off with more dash than the first time.

To-day I have been over a large store; it is of vast size, and every description of merchandise is sold—all wearing-apparel, male and female, from boots to hats, all kind of ironmongers' stores, wines and beer—in fact, there is hardly a thing you can mention that they do not sell—wool, ostrich feathers, and all colonial produce. There are hydraulic lifts from one floor to the other, three hydraulic presses for pressing wool—two tons to the square inch, which ought to quash most bales into shape. Then they have their own repairing shop, steam saw-mills, and a carriage department. Stores of this kind are, I think, peculiar to the Cape Colony: in Australia, and elsewhere, stores confine themselves more to one sort of article. I was surprised to hear that Cape Colony and Natal import more English goods than Canada or any other English colony—£6,000,000 worth a-year. I saw it in the report of the Port Elizabeth Chamber of Commerce, so there is no mistake about it; but I will not inflict you with any figures, as these can be got from blue-books; and yet this is the colony that the present Government speak so slightingly of. Just recently there have been nine steamers lying in Algoa Bay, with a total tonnage of twenty thousand, besides sailing-ships.

There is no doubt that if the Government, instead of patching up treaties with the old countries in Europe on unfavourable terms, would do something in the way of a new basis of commercial tariffs with the whole of the colonies, it would be far better, as growing and increasing countries like the colonies are much more worth fostering;

they must progress, and in Australia and other colonies, America and Germany are going ahead wonderfully in the way of cutting England out of her own natural markets. The colonists are loyal enough, but this Transvaal business has upset the idea that when England promised, by the mouth of her General and by the Government, that loyal subjects should be protected, they would be; and it will take a good deal to change the idea which is prevalent that the present Government wish to cut the colonies adrift. Of course we know that this is an exaggerated idea, but it is the general one out here amongst people of both sides of politics. I see the Kaffirs naturally say that if the English give the Transvaal back to the Boers, who took it from the natives, that it ought to be given back to the original owners; and in that they are quite right.

CHAPTER XV.

ELEPHANTS.

Port Elizabeth,
August 14*th*, 1881.

On Tuesday last I dined with a Mr. Blackburn, and heard that at the big "shoot" I was invited to last Saturday week good sport was had, and that several bucks and other game were killed. On Wednesday G — and I started for Grahamstown. We had a six-hours' railway journey, for the first half of the time through a dense bush, in which there are elephants; they are strictly preserved, and there is a very heavy penalty for shooting them. We then gradually ascended, and had some very fine views of mountain scenery, and arrived at the station just at twilight. Like all hotels in South Africa, the one we went to was nearly full, and we had a small double-bedded room allotted to us. In the morning it was raining and blowing with hurricane force—a great nuisance.

Grahamstown is a place of some ten thousand inhabitants, situated in a hollow, with low hills all round, and as there are a good many trees about, it gives a pleasant look to the place, for trees are doubtless the great want in South Africa. It is called the "City of the Saints," and is noted for its churches, chapels, and schools. The Courts of Justice are here, and although it has no trade like Port Elizabeth, it is a fairly lively place, and the society, I hear, pleasant. The cathedral is a rather curious building; it has a magnificent stone spire, built from the designs of Sir Gilbert Scott, with a very fine peal of bells; the spire alone cost £10,000, and is the only part of the design carried out. The rest of the building is the old Dutch Church, a whitewashed barn affair, and very incongruous it looks. However, everything has a beginning, and like Cologne Cathedral, they live in hopes of its being completed, though let us hope it will not be six hundred years before it is finished. As is too common out here, there is division in the Church, and the Bishop and the Dean are at "daggers drawn"—a most unfortunate circumstance.

It appears that in England the Bishop in his

own diocese can only preach in the cathedral at the Sunday morning service, and appoint preachers for that service, the Dean and Chapter having the right to appoint preachers for the other services, for all services on saints' days, and on special occasions; in fact, the Bishop cannot preach in his own cathedral other than in the morning, except by invitation of the Dean and Chapter. I suppose that is the reason why, in the morning, preachers at St. Paul's are often Low Church, and in the evening nearly invariably High; for with such men as Dean Church and Canons Gregory and Liddon in the Chapter, of course High Church preachers are selected by them. Anyhow, one Sunday the Bishop said he was going to preach in the cathedral; the Dean said he should not, without his permission; so on the Sunday the Dean, with unseemly haste, mounted the pulpit and gave out his text, while the Bishop of Grahamstown was on his way there. The latter, seeing the Dean in possession, merely walked out, and has not been in the cathedral since. It has been twice decided against the Bishop out here, but he has appealed to England, and in the meantime the Dean is in undisputed possession, the Bishop doing duty at Christ Church. The whole town, in fact the whole diocese, is divided, some going with the Bishop and some with the Dean. It certainly is a great pity that the ecclesiastical law appears so uncertain, as it is ruinous to the welfare of the Church.

The church that Uncle J — goes to has not been consecrated, and is under no jurisdiction, though the Bishop preaches there by invitation, as not only is there a squabble about the services in the cathedral, but some years ago the Government of the day agreed that in future, with the exception of the Bishop of Cape Town, who was to come from England, all the bishops in South Africa were to be selected from men in the Church in South Africa, and chosen by the Bishop of Cape Town, but there was some informality about the proceedings. The Bishop of Grahamstown was one of the first appointed under the new Act, and some people say he is not a bishop at all. The Dean had been appointed by the English Government, so I fancy he is all correct.

We hired two horses, and rode eleven miles to a farm, where a friend of G—'s resides; we had a lovely ride. The mountain scenery reminded me somewhat of Wales—torrents foaming by, and vegetation very fine, masses of arums growing wild, and numerous other flowering shrubs. It blew hard, but we reached Sevenoaks without rain, and had a feast of guavas, loquats, and other fruits. Oranges, figs, apples, all flourish here in the season, also turnips and all English vegetables; masses of roses and heliotropes; and this in winter; they also had some ostriches, and I quite enjoyed the day's out. Mrs. W—, the wife of the owner, is a very pretty Jewish matron, wrapped up in her first-born, an intelligent boy of eighteen months. Her husband was at the Bay, but S— did the honours. He was nearly killed the other day by an ostrich. They are very savage at present, as it is their breeding season, and they run at you like greased lightning, and kick at you with one of their powerful legs, at the end of which are huge claws. So narrow an escape had young S—, that his breeches were torn, but his flesh was not scratched. I believe the best way is to throw yourself flat down on the ground, as then they have more difficulty in striking you. We stayed to lunch, and rode back in pelting rain, with wind of hurricane force.

Next morning, though blowing hard, we set off to ride again ; we missed the road, and went five or six miles out of our way. We then had a ten-mile ride to a place called Roby, on the way to the Kowie. We saw splendid avenues of trees, and, owing to the clouds, the hills looked very fine with their ever-changing colours, and we could see miles and miles of undulating plains ; in fact, a very grand panorama. We arrived in time for dinner.

On Saturday we rode out again to Sevenoaks, intending to stop the night, but two horses had strayed, so S— and his companions had to go in search of them, for if they once get away in the bush, it may take days to find them. We stayed lunch, and rode back after being all over the ostrich paddocks again ; and though it was only where very young ones are that we ventured, still I was not happy, as a young cock bird, with his stupid-looking head, gazed after us ; and when once started, with their enormous strides, they are on you in a moment. The only safeguard is, that, curious to relate, a fence two or three feet high keeps them at bay, or even a narrow ditch appears to make them quite flurried ; anything bright attracts them, and buttons they soon take off your coat, unless you are on the look-out.

Yesterday we went to the cathedral. The Dean who has a voice like thunder, gave us a remarkably fine address on the education of the young. He is a powerful preacher, and, physically, an awkward man to tackle. The text was the 54th of Isaiah and the 13th verse. He referred incidentally to the remarkable fact that the late Lord Hatherley, Lord Cairns, and Lord Selborne had all been Sunday-school teachers. The Botanical Gardens are not open on Sundays, but we got in a back way easy enough; the getting out was the question. We had to climb a huge iron gate, with spikes; this is Sabbatarianism with a vengeance. In the afternoon we went to Wood's Grotto, and very pretty it was, the ferns and variegated leaves being very fine; the stalactites and the stalagmites, though artificial, were most natural. People, when they have retired from business, come to Grahamstown to live, the climate being cooler than at Port Elizabeth. In the evening we heard the author of "Orthodox and Unorthodox London," and other books, preach. He has thirteen children, poor man, so will make a good colonist. He is coming out to some school connected with the cathedral. We left Grahamstown at 10 p.m., and reached here this morning at 6 a.m., after a pleasant four days' trip.

There is no doubt that you see more English here than in Cape Town, and there are not so many "snuff and butters" as in other parts of the country. "Snuff and butters" is the term for half-castes; rather good, I think, for cover butter with pepper or snuff, and you have about their complexion. The English ladies here have not much colour, as the sea air and the hot, moist atmosphere of summer whitens them. In Grahamstown, which is seventeen hundred feet high, rosy cheeks are all the rage.

I have been, and am going to be, very gay this week—out every evening; in fact, the people are all very hospitable and pleasant, but just as you get to know them, one is leaving. The weather here has been very changeable of late, but there have been some fine bright days between the storms. Just returned from a delightful drive of two hours and a half with Mr. Blackburn, who took two gentlemen and myself to a very fine ostrich farm, one of the largest in the colony. In one huge enclosure there were no fewer than a hundred young birds, and eighty pairs in separate paddocks. The cock bird sits as well as the hen, and they say that their regularity is wonderful; if, for instance, the cock bird begins to sit at 4 p.m., he is relieved by his faithful partner at 4 the next morning. If anything goes wrong with the nest, the incubator is used. Pairs of ostriches at four years old are worth from £160 to £300, as that is the year they begin to breed, and they live to great ages, so you may imagine that the value of this farm is considerable; it is six thousand acres in extent. The birds are plucked every ten months, and have several broods in the year; the spring and autumn ones are the best. An ostrich may lay from thirty to forty eggs a year. They pay well with good luck, but they are subject to a great many diseases. The feathers of the tame birds are not so valuable as those of the wild ones, the supposition being that the food given is not of the right kind, and that they get something in their wild state that they do not get when brought up artificially; but doubtless this will be rectified with experience. £1,000,000 worth of ostrich feathers were exported last year, and as the trade is just commencing, it is wonderful to think of the success of the undertaking; but, like all things started suddenly, it is being overdone, and people who know no more about the habits of the birds than I do have started ostrich farms, and have been ruined in consequence; legitimately carried out, however, it is doubtless a paying concern.

One or two companies that started ostrich farming have smashed up. To begin with, they stated in their prospectus that they had so many eggs, and drew it up on the basis that each egg would produce a chicken; which, in the case of ostriches, was certainly an example of counting your chickens before they are hatched, as they are most uncertain birds, and if disturbed will break all the eggs in the nest. They further valued each chicken that was to be hatched at £5, and when the chickens that did survive the dangers of hatching arrived, their market value for the time had gone down to 30s., so the company practically burst up. I know two young friends of mine who had bought, say, £10 shares at par, and found they were hardly worth as much as the paper they were written on.

Like other speculations, ostrich farming needs capital to weather bad seasons, and the personal supervision of the owner of the farm, to be successful. Companies with a manager are, I hear, not likely to do well. Incubators were at first tried a good deal, but it is found that the birds thus hatched are weakly. A number of sheep runs have been turned into ostrich farms, and for a year or so it will do the land no harm—in fact, improve it, as ostriches clear the ground of coarse grass and weeds that the sheep will not touch; but in the end sheep farming will pay best, as wool is the staple of South Africa, and people will always want clothing, unless climates change, while ostrich feathers are more subject to the freaks of fashion. Each pair of ostriches require seven to nine acres of ground fenced in, and, in addition to what they pick up, are regularly fed on mealies, lucern grass, bones, &c. The profits on ostrich farming necessarily fluctuate with the value of feathers in the European markets.

As anticipated in a former letter, I see that General Wood has had to go to Zululand, as there is great bloodshed there. It is ignominious to hear that they do not care a rap for the English residents, but for John Dunn everything. Of course this is the outcome of the Transvaal fiasco. Natives only respect the most powerful nation for the time being. They think the Dutch are the conquerors, and since coming home, I see the Government of the Transvaal are indicating their intention of conciliating the natives; and already signs are manifest that the native tribes of the interior, having lost confidence in England, are disposed to make terms with the Boers; and Joubert's expressions of a desire for Cetewayo's return is regarded as aiming at weakening England's prestige amongst the natives. Unfortunately, so far as I can hear, it is *gone already.*

We are having very fine weather again now, the thermometer standing at 70 degrees. The bathing in the morning is delightful; such splendid breakers! in fact, it is regular surf bathing, as one dare not go out into deep water, owing to the sharks.

As I sail next week for England, this will be my last letter, and I can safely advise those who want a bracing trip of three months, to come out here any time from May to the end of August, as there is nearly a perfect climate, a new country, and yet some places historically interesting. Owing to the late wars, the Cape Colony is becoming more known in England; but to give you an idea how little was known of it, even on the London Exchange, a few years ago, I will tell you a story of a gentleman—a friend of mine, hailing from Algoa Bay—who was introduced in London to a merchant. After speaking to my friend, the latter, turning round to his companion, said, " Why, dear me, he is almost white ! "

I left Port Elizabeth in a storm of rain and wind, in the " Pretoria," for Cape Town, and we arrived in Table Bay in thirty-one hours, or an average of fourteen knots and a quarter. We certainly had a south-east wind with us, but it was good going. I landed, and went to the Royal Hotel, and spent the afternoon at Wynberg.

On Monday I dined with B —, and afterwards went to hear the "Pirates of Penzance." I described the scenery about Cape Town when I was here before, so shall not repeat, and as I am going home the same route I came out by, I shall not attempt to say anything more of the voyage than that we sailed from Cape Town on Tuesday, the 30th of August, at 4.50 p.m., for England, eight hours after the unfortunate "Teuton" had left for the eastward. We had a lovely start, bright moonlight and a calm sea, and the latter we carried with us all the way to Plymouth, which we reached at 4 a.m. on the 18th of September, or, including stoppages at St. Helena and Madeira, a run of 18 days, 11 hours, 15 minutes. The actual steaming time was 18 days, 5 hours, 50 minutes. The distance is about 6,000 miles, therefore it was a daily average of 329 miles. The "Pretoria," on this occasion, made the fastest voyage on record. It was the perfection of ocean travelling, never having had the ports closed the whole way, and the two stoppages at St. Helena and Madeira broke the monotony of the voyage. We had pleasant passengers, and "what could you wish for more?" It was a brilliant wind-up to a successful trip, and I shall always look back to my three months' tour in South Africa with pleasure.

I landed at Plymouth, and a prettier harbour on a bright day in Autumn it would be difficult to find. The breakwater, the ironclads, the wooded slopes of Mount Edgecumbe, Drake's Island, and the town itself, made a *tout ensemble* one seldom sees. Though I enjoyed seeing the wonders of Africa, and the drives over the Karoo, which, for vastness, resembles a mighty ocean with boundless horizon, yet my ride in the train to Exeter convinced me of the fact that nothing can compare with the quiet beauty and true pastoral scenery of England.

LIVERPOOL:
ADAM HOLDEN, PRINTER,
CHURCH STREET.

www.ingramcontent.com/pod-product-compliance
Lightning Source LLC
Chambersburg PA
CBHW020909230426
43666CB00008B/1375